MW00780847

FRONT LINE LEADERSHIP

APPLYING MILITARY STRATEGIES
TO EVERYDAY BUSINESS

NICHOLAS R. RIPPLINGER

Front Line Leadership:
Applying Military Strategies to Everyday Business
By Nicholas R. Ripplinger

Copyright © 2016 by Nicholas R. Ripplinger

Cover Design by Melodye Hunter

ISBN: 978-1-944177-19-5 (p)
ISBN: 978-1-944177-20-1 (e)

Crescendo Publishing, LLC
300 Carlsbad Village Drive
Ste. 108A, #443
Carlsbad, California 92008-2999

www.CrescendoPublishing.com
GetPublished@CrescendoPublishing.com

This book has undergone a Department of Defense Security Review. All requested changes have been fully incorporated, and this publication is compliant with all Department of Defense requirements.

A Message from the Author:

Download a complimentary Lost Chapter
"The Board: Round 2" here:

http://www.nickripplinger.com/

Dedication

This book is dedicated to my two sons, Silas and Lucas. I hope I have shown you both, through my actions, how to be a great leader and that this book can be a reference for you in times of need when I am no longer here.

This book is also dedicated to the men and women in uniform who are fighting for my freedom to be able to write this book. I cannot thank you all enough.

Foreword

Thank you Nick Ripplinger for writing the book that needed to be written.Having the honor to work with those in our Armed Forces I have come to realize how powerful their training and discipline is, and how it translates so well into being successful when they transition into the business world.

Nick brilliantly in this book shows what true leadership is. I hope if you are an employer this book opens your eyes to the qualities a veteran can bring to your company that goes far beyond a college education.

If you are a veteran, I hope this book opens your eyes to how powerful your experiences in the military are and has prepared you to be a ROCK STAR in the business world.

When you discover the gifts your experiences have been and use these experiences to move you forward in a positive direction life becomes brighter not only for you but all those around you.

Dave Austin
~Author of the International best-selling book "Be A Beast" and founder of Extreme Focus

Table of Contents

Introduction

*"There are no secrets to success.
It is the result of preparation, hard
work, and learning from failure."*

— Colin Powell

So many veterans, like myself, have struggled with the transition from military life to civilian life. The most common complaint I have heard is "nothing I have done or learned in the military translates to the business world." The second-most common complaint is "I never had the time to complete my formal education between deployments, training, and all the other stupid things I was tasked with." Both of these complaints are fairly valid for most enlisted veterans.

No employer has ever asked for my extensive military training records or a list of the countless correspondence courses I took for a few extra promotion points. I have, however, been asked to provide official copies of my transcripts from an accredited university from time to time. I will be the first to admit that I did not take full advantage of the tuition-reimbursement program while I was serving, partly because I deployed multiple times, went on field-training exercises often, and did not want to miss a night with the boys before or after these events. But most of all, I just did not see the value of a formal education while I was serving. To add to that, I still believe that real-life experiences trumps formal education every day.

As for the transferable skills, I picked up on that fairly quickly. Most events in life are transferable and marketable as long as you can pull the meaning from the event and know how to connect and apply the meaning to the business realm. The first time I connected the dots was back when I was a young Private and did something stupid that landed me a position on the Battalion Command Sergeant Major's cleanup crew. I was pushing a broken-down lawn mower—in brand-new boots, I might add—and I remember saying to myself, "Now I'm a skilled grass-height manager." Over the course of about two acres, it became a game of sorts to think of all the undesirable tasks the United States Army assigned me and how I could civilianize these newly acquired skills. At this time in my life, I was a young Private First Class, so the majority of my skills involved cleaning something, such as "professional mirror-spot remover" or "professional cigarette-butt picker-upper." I thought these skills would be great job titles to use while trying to pick up women when they asked me what I did for a living (although I am sure my haircut gave me away in a military town). I also thought these skills would one day enable me to open my own cleaning company, or at least I would excel on the local jail roadside cleaning crew. Thankfully, none of these three ideas ever panned out for me.

Living in the barracks can be lonely at times. Let's face it: there is only so much beer one can drink. So every night after work and dinner, I sat down to think about what I did that day and how I could translate that to the "business world." (Now would probably be a good time to mention that I never planned to get out of the United States Army and start a civilian career. I wanted to stay in until they forced me to retire after thirty-some-odd years, but that plan didn't quite work out for me.) Some nights I had several practical, translatable experiences and lessons learned. Other nights all I had was "master of dirt removal" from a gravel parking lot. Yes, one time I had to sweep a gravel parking lot. However, as the years went by and I earned a little more rank, I gained more meaningful experiences and transferable skills that I was able to apply to my civilian career in business.

The most meaningful lessons I learned and that stayed with me were those about leadership— the one thing that can kill the morale and productivity in an organization. It also seems to be the biggest element lacking in most businesses. Don't get me wrong: there are some amazing business leaders out there who strive to do what is right by their people and who constantly do everything in their power to become a better leader. (In this "me" culture, however, so many people who call themselves leaders are looking out only for themselves and don't care about anything but the next promotion. This is completely unacceptable and totally preventable as you will see in the following chapters.)

Leadership is something that can be taught or learned through life experiences as long as we are willing to seek out these experiences and learn from them. Some of the skills and lessons I learned were things I was taught or figured out on my own after being ordered to do something. Others I picked up on by watching other soldiers, or listening to their stories and overanalyzing them (like I do with nearly everything in life). All of these stories are true and documented to the best of my memory, but like I said, some of them were pulled from others. This is not intended to be my autobiography but stories from my experiences that have helped shape me into the person and leader I have become over the years.

Some terms, acronyms, military ranks, or other sayings might not be familiar to you if you are not a veteran. No worries though. We do have our own language, but it is a lot easier than English. I have tried my best to describe these potentially uncommon words inside the chapters where they fall.

These stories are in chronological order from the time I entered the United States Army in March of 2004 until my career ended in March of 2011. I tried my best to identify what year these experiences happened, but in some of the chapters they are rough estimates.

Chapter 1
Basic Training

*"You will never be a leader unless
you first learn to follow and be led."*

— Tiorio

In the summer of 2004, between my junior and
senior years of high school, I got my first taste of real-
life United States Army leadership. During this time I
spent ten long weeks getting broken down and built
back up in the United States Army's vision of a soldier
at basic training in the summer heat of Fort Leonard
Wood, Missouri.

Basic training was a very special, invaluable time of
my life, during which I got to experience a lot of things
for the first time. I got to shoot a machine gun, rappel
off a building, and walk fifteen miles for no reason while
a pickup truck followed us. But most importantly, it was

my first experience with military leadership, which was not at all what I expected.

During basic training, the Drill Sergeants used fear, repetition, and reprisals to teach us the basic combat skills that molded us into soldiers and that could one day save our lives or the lives of others in the combat theaters of Iraq and Afghanistan. There were countless push-ups, sit-ups, flutter kicks, and a myriad of other exercises that I have successfully blocked from my memory. To this day I am still not sure if any of those exercises made me a better war fighter or not. However, it was what we all had to do to earn the honor of calling ourselves United States Army soldiers.

During the majority of basic training, especially the first several weeks, we couldn't do a damn thing right. I am serious. We couldn't even use the bathroom correctly. Even if we were able to do something right, someone in our company would not do it correctly and that was when the yelling and throwing things started. We all knew that the Drill Sergeants were not allowed to hit us, but we all had a fear that at some point we were going to get hit by something or someone. This fear kept all of us on our toes, but it never allowed for the whole team to be successful. Some soldiers used this fear as motivation, while others allowed it to stress them out almost to the point of a mental and physical breakdown.

We feared the Drill Sergeants for other reasons besides the whole physical-harm thing. We all were fearful that we would be the one to make a mistake that caused everyone to be in the front-leaning-rest position or doing some other form of exercise. We did not want to let our battle buddies down, but we knew someone would make a mistake. I damn sure didn't want it to be me, and I am sure others felt the same way. This fear of failure ate at the majority of us the whole time—we were all terrified of the Drill Sergeants for some reason or another.

Please, do not get me wrong. I am not putting down basic training here at all. Like I said, I had a blast during this time of my life, and I would do it all over again in a heartbeat if I could. The experience of basic training will always hold a special place in my heart for all the lessons I learned.

I would not trust myself to throw a grenade or to clear a room in an urban combat theater today, but right after basic training I would have trusted myself and everyone with whom I graduated. So the Army knows what they are doing when it comes to basic training, and it works for a military organization. However, if we employ the same fear tactics in business, without a doubt, we will fail miserably.

Businesses need to be run by instilling respect and confidence and not by fear. When you lead with fear, people are afraid to speak their minds. This means that someone on your team could have the next big idea that expands your company or takes you to a place you could only dream of, but they will not speak up and share their ideas simply because they are afraid of being belittled in front of their peers. A team will also not be nearly as productive as they could be because team members will always be looking over their shoulders, waiting to get stabbed in the back, whether it is a valid fear or not. This fear is unhealthy for individuals but even more devastating for a team environment as it breaks down much-needed trust among team members. In addition, fear makes employees hide mistakes because they don't feel comfortable bringing them to leadership's attention. In turn, this creates larger problems down the road as smaller issues are swept under the rug, turning into bigger issues later.

We cannot let ourselves be feared by our team if we truly want to be considered a leader and run a successful project, team, or business. We have to conduct ourselves in a way that is nurturing, caring, open, and dedicated to creating a culture of creativity and collaboration if we ever want ourselves and our team to reach our full potential.

Chapter 2
Grid Squares

*"The most important single ingredient
in the formula of success is knowing
how to get along with people."*

— Theodore Roosevelt

Luckily this story did not happen to me, but it very easily could have, had I not taken an extra thirty seconds in the latrine (restrooms) to bum a pinch of Grizzly mint off another soldier.

We had just returned from eating lunch in the DFAC (dining facility), and there really wasn't much for us to do. The same was true for the NCOs (Non-Commissioned Officers E5 to E9), but when there was downtime, NCOs tended to enjoy messing with the heads of the young Privates assigned to them. A new Sergeant to the company (and probably the Army) called for the nearest Private and told him to go down to battalion supply and sign out a box of grid squares.

I didn't pay much attention to what was going on, but I do remember thinking two things: the first was that I needed to find a good hiding spot to avoid being tasked with something that stupid, and the second was what the hell was a grid square? I knew that a map was comprised of a series of lines that created a grid system, and the individual boxes were called "grid squares," which were used to identify positions on a map, but that was about all I knew about it.

So a few hours go by, and the Sergeant got a call from the Battalion Supply Sergeant telling him to quit wasting his time on "fuck-fuck games." Another hour passed with still no sign of the Private. The young Private finally made his return and with a box full of grid squares. He proceeded to dump the box of grid squares on the Sergeant's desk. The Sergeant asked the soldier, "Where the hell did you get these?" The Private explained that supply was out of grid squares, but the Battalion Command Sergeant Major had a map on his desk. Because the map was still intact, the Private had to cut the map into squares to accomplish the mission and bring back grid squares. The Sergeant then ran off, and I could only assume he was planning a one-way trip to a country without extradition for the simple fact that you do not mess with a Battalion Command Sergeant Major without receiving a very heavy-handed repercussion.

I hope this funny story gave you a chuckle or two, but there are several good life lessons that happened here that can very easily translate into the business world. The first lesson I took away from this was that no matter how slow things can be from time to time, coming up with busy work is never the answer to keeping employees occupied. This would have been a great time for some on-the-spot training and mentoring. I am sure there was also something in the motor pool that needed a good cleaning.

The second lesson is one that I did not learn right away after this happened, but you will see other examples of it later on in this book: If you are going to play a joke or have some fun around the office or workplace, make sure that everyone is fully aware of what is going on or what is about to happen. There is no need for a joke to go as far as hurting another organization's or department's productivity. We were about to deploy, and the battalion supply team was extremely busy gathering and inventorying all the gear we would need to take with us down range. There was really no time to waste at this point of the deployment prep, and this prank did just that.

The third lesson comes from the young Private. It is probably the most notable of this story and continues to help me in my post-military career. Before I explain, let me tell you something that is not called out in the story. The Battalion Supply Sergeant told the Private that going for grid squares was a stupid game that some NCOs liked to play on young soldiers. The Private laughed it off and instantly went into revenge mode. He asked the supply Sergeant what he could do to mess with the Sergeant without getting smoked (a series of exercises to help correct a situation) to death. The supply Sergeant went next door to the training Sergeant and asked for a Tenino map. I am not really sure of the story behind the Tenino map, but it has just about every land feature on it, so it is a common map-reading training aid. The supply Sergeant gave the map to the Private and told him to cut out all the grid squares and tell his NCO that it was the map on the Battalion Command Sergeant Major's desk.

The Private could have just licked his wounds and returned to the company motor pool, but instead he started a conversation with the supply Sergeant. That conversation led to a great connection and eventually a strong friendship. The young Private somehow ended up with the best gear that deployment as well. Never let a connection pass you by because you never know what that connection can turn into down the road or how beneficial it can be to either party.

The fourth lesson learned here also comes from the Private. However, in this case the Private didn't follow this advice: Always do as much research as possible before accepting a task. Now granted, we did not have iPhones back then, but a quick question to one of the members of the E4 mafia (military slang for a group of Specialists) he passed on his way to the battalion supply room could have prevented this whole story. Sometimes just asking a simple question can keep you from looking incredibly incompetent.

The fifth and final lesson from this story comes from the Sergeant again. If you task someone with something stupid, expect an insanely stupid outcome. This is something I always consider before asking anyone to do something for me, which in business, translates to adding value to what you are trying to accomplish. So if you ask yourself, "Does this add value to the project, department, or organization?" and you get a "yes" or even a "somewhat," then assign the task. Remember, time is money, and you do not want any team member to feel that their time and the company's money is wasted. The thing to remember when assigning a task is to make sure you provide enough resources—anything from time, capital, or something as simple as providing all the required information for the task at hand—for the employee to successfully accomplish the task.

Chapter 3
The Essay

"Setting goals is the first step in turning the invisible into the visible."

— Tony Robbins

Back in 2005, I was the Brigade Commander's driver. One of the responsibilities that the Brigade Commander had was to administer Article 15 hearings, which is a non-judicial punishment for troops who have violated the Uniform Code of Military Justice or UCMJ. When a soldier is facing UCMJ action, their whole leadership chain of command must be present for the hearing. Just to make it a little more uncomfortable for everyone involved, the hearings were usually held at 1730 (5:30 p.m.) on a Friday evening. I also had to be present for these hearings to make sure everything went smoothly out in the lobby before and after the hearing. I got this job because my desk was located in the lobby.

The Brigade Command Sergeant Major would always show up early and spend a good chunk of time talking to me while he waited for the soldier and the rest of the leadership team to show up. He would always tell me that as long as I did things right, I would never find myself in the same situation as the troops in the hearings. He would also make small talk by asking about my family and what I had going on in my personal life. The Command Sergeant Major always took the extra step to get to know the soldiers who served under him.

On this particular day he asked me what my one- and five-year goals were. I distinctly remember giving him a blank stare and basically saying that I didn't really know. The Command Sergeant Major responded, "Damn, Ripplinger, I thought you were smarter than that." He also explained that I was going to meet him the next morning (Saturday) at 0900 (9:00 a.m.) with an essay documenting my professional goals.

I stayed up until about 0200 (2:00 a.m.) working on my essay that stated my goals and why they were important to me both professionally and personally. I won't lie; it was not my best writing, but the content and reasoning behind my goals were extremely solid.

That night I got a few hours of sleep and showed up at the office at 0830 (8:30 a.m.), because in the military if you are early, you are on time, and if you are on time, you are late. The fact that the Command Sergeant Major did not care for tardiness also played into my decision to show up thirty minutes early. At exactly 0900 (9:00 a.m.), the Command Sergeant Major called me into his office. With a prideful smile, I handed over my six-page handwritten essay. The Command Sergeant Major took my document, turned around in his chair, and began to shred my document without reading a single word. I tried to stop him, but I was quickly called to the position of attention, a position where you cannot speak. After he finished shredding the document one page at a time, he turned back around and asked one simple question: "What can I do to help you achieve your goals?"

The biggest thing I learned from the Command Sergeant Major is that we all have goals. Some of us know specifically what and where we want to be while others have a more general sense of what they want. But the Command Sergeant Major showed me the importance of documentation. Talk is pretty cheap, but when you create a document by putting pen to paper, you have now created something that you can use to help keep yourself accountable—to help you achieve what you want in your career and, more importantly, in your life.

Personally, my goals have changed several times since I wrote that essay, and many more times throughout my career. This is totally normal and it is a good thing. Whenever my life starts going in a different direction, or when I learn or figure out something new that sparks my interest and sends me down a different path, I open up my goals document and make the appropriate changes. I also know that reviewing your objectives on a regular basis is key to achieving your goals. As a practice, I review my one-, three-, five-, and ten-year objectives every Monday and come up with tasks for the week that will help move me consistently forward toward achieving my goals.

As leaders we are all driven and probably already know the value of documenting our goals. But in my opinion, it is just as important (if not more so) that we know our team members' goals. I have always had my soldiers and employees provide me with a list of their goals, although not in an essay format. I do this so that I am fully aware of where they want to go and how I can help them achieve their goals. As leaders, very similar to parents, we should want our team (like our children) to be more successful than we were when we were in their shoes. When you care for and respect people, you have a passion for helping them achieve everything they want in life. In order for us as leaders to get them to the finish line, we have to know their goals and the motivation behind their goals.

Chapter 4
New Job

*"If you're not actively involved in
getting what you want, you don't
really want it."*

— Peter McWilliams

The military is very structured when it comes to almost everything, especially jobs and assignments. I can remember very clearly three times during my military career when I was not happy with my current job or assignment, so I took actions to create a new job for myself.

As a very young, motivated Private back in 2005, all I wanted to do was deploy. After all, I did enlist after 9/11 because I wanted to fight back and defend our country. However, that is not what good ole Uncle Sam had in store for me. Instead, I was assigned to the brigade headquarters as the secondary driver to the Brigade Commander—just about the worst job I could ever hold. I was responsible for making sure someone else was on time and where he needed to be at all times. At that time I might have been eighteen years old and couldn't even do that for myself. One thing that has remained consistent with me though is that I have always hated the idea of being a secondary anything.

So I set two goals. The first goal was to become the primary driver, and the second was to get the hell out of the headquarters, find a slot to deploy, and go fight in Iraq or Afghanistan. The first goal was easy because I had some help. The primary driver had his fill of being the Commander's driver and was ready for a change. The primary driver and I completed his transfer paperwork and waited for the Commander to go on travel. While a Commander is on travel, his deputy usually has the same authority and the ability to sign for the Commander. This is very beneficial when you need something signed that you know the Commander would never sign. So the deputy signed the transfer forms, and the primary driver was gone before the boss was back. I was now the primary driver, but it was still not the job I really wanted.

So I had to come up with a way to no longer be the primary driver. The first step was training a suitable replacement because I did not want the Commander to have to drive himself to the Officer's Club or the golf course. The command team pulled the next Private from the bottom to come train to be the secondary driver. It took two weeks to train him, and then it was time to make my exit. (I might mention that a sneak attack while the Commander was gone was not an option this time around. Apparently that is something you can do only once.)

I remembered an old Sergeant First Class that used to work in our building who had been recently promoted to First Sergeant. He was taking his guys down range to Iraq, and I remembered that he always complimented me on my motivation. I reached out to him to help me make this whole thing happen.

To make a very long story short, this is how it went: I spoke to the First Sergeant, he made a phone call to the Command Sergeant Major, I got yelled at by the Commander, I got the transfer, I got the job I wanted, I deployed. What I just summed up in a few lines took only a few days. It's amazing how fast things can go when you have the right people on your team.

The second time I created my own job was back in 2008. I was a new Sergeant and at a new base, so no one knew me or what I was capable of doing. As a new Sergeant I wanted to lead troops and have my own team. That's usually how it goes in the military; however, sometimes things do not go as planned. There were five other Sergeants to my right and two Staff Sergeants. I was certainly not getting a team anytime soon because the military theory is to wait your time, and time in grade (how long you have been a certain rank) trumps everything.

My personal theory on this subject is that the best performers will have people requesting to work for them. So the first time we did physical training as a team, I tried to outperform the rest of the leaders. I came in third out of seven leaders, and I figured I'd take that. I knew that I didn't have to be the best at every aspect of soldiering, but if I was near the top in every area and if I had no major areas of weakness, I knew I would be just fine.

We spent many long hours working in the motor pool at that unit, so I spent a lot of time and energy trying to figure out what the senior leaders wanted done around the motor pool. I did work that was not assigned but that I knew would be requested at some point, probably after it was time to go home. This allowed us to go home on time, and the troops noticed who was making this happen. All the sudden, guess who was the new team leader? If you guessed me, you are correct. The soldiers requested to work for me, and I had already proven myself so it was a no-brainer for the leadership. I am going to add that my annual review looked great, as I was chosen to lead over five others who were more "experienced"—or at least who should have been more experienced due to their time in grade.

The third time I made my own position was in 2010 while assigned to the European Command. About six years after my first job in the military, I was selected to be a driver again, this time for a Combatant Commander, or a Four-Star General. This is much higher than a Brigade Commander, but nevertheless, I still didn't want to be someone's driver, so I decided I wasn't going to be. I had done this once, so I didn't see a reason why I couldn't make the change again.

At this point in my life, I was now married and wanting to start a family, so deploying again was not ideal. (Although it wouldn't have been ideal, without a doubt I would have fought with pride if I got orders to deploy. After all, that was what I signed up for back in

2004.) I also had already suffered my combat-related leg injury, so going back to the regular Army wasn't a great option either. Regardless, I was simply not cut out to be a secretary or some other enlisted aide to a very important officer.

Now knowing what I did not want to do, I set up a meeting with the detachment Non-Commissioned Officer in Charge (NCOIC) to see what he needed in his detachment. You will read more about him in chapter 24, "The Mentor." He told me that he needed help on the operations side, but he had already selected a Staff Sergeant to fill that position. (FYI ... I was still a Sergeant at this time, and it is the norm that the second-highest in rank is the Operations NCOIC, but I was about to change that.) I started taking on tasks around the detachment that would have normally fallen to the Operations NCOIC. I did this for about two weeks, and before you knew it, the Staff Sergeant was the primary driver, and I was the Operations NCOIC. It's funny how all that worked out.

In life and in business you won't always be given what you want. There may be some people along the way willing to help you out, but you will never be spoon-fed exactly what you are looking for. You have to create the job and projects you want in business. Sometimes this means eliminating some tasks or responsibilities, or picking up additional tasks and responsibilities that you want.

You first have to identity what it is that you want in life, both personally and professionally. The next step is to come up with a plan for how you are going to achieve your goals. Remember, you don't have to do everything on your own; you can bring in a team of people who all have the same goals and mindset to increase your chances for success. It is also vital to remain flexible and open-minded because sometimes opportunities present themselves that you did not plan on but that you could benefit from.

In your career whether it be military, civilian, employee, or entrepreneur, you are going to have to create your own job at some point in your career. It may be to save your position from a layoff, it could be that you don't want to tread water and you want to grow, or it could be that you flat-out don't want to drive a grown man around. Whatever the reasons, you must have a clear vision for what you are trying to achieve and a path to achieve the vision. Do not take your eye off the prize for a second.

One of the biggest elements about being a leader is that we always have to look for ways to improve ourselves. In the three short stories in this chapter, all my new jobs were a step up in my career, and they challenged me. When we decide to move on from one position, we have to make sure we are going toward something and not just running away from our current situation. We have to always seek continuous improvement for our personal and professional lives. This comes in many different forms, such as taking classes or gaining new mentors, and sometimes it is making a change in our employment situation.

Chapter 5
FTX

*"The people when rightly and fully
trusted will return the trust."*

— Abraham Lincoln

In early 2006 we were on a field-training exercise to help us prepare for our upcoming deployment to Iraq in just a few months. During a field-training exercise we would spend two to three weeks out in the woods and conduct both day and night operations. Some soldiers like myself loved this type of training while others despised these types of exercises. I think all soldiers felt one of these two extremes, leaving very little gray area.

Most soldiers do well during the first week of a field-training exercise because they are not exhausted or absolutely disgusting by this time. The soldiers who hate field-training exercises start to show their frustration around the second week of training. On the second week of this particular field-training exercise, we had a newly promoted Sergeant assigned as a team leader to our squad. I was walking back to our tent when I noticed that the new Sergeant had half the squad—consisting of five or six junior soldiers—locked up in the position of parade rest. He was chewing into them for not listening to him and for not respecting his authority as a Sergeant.

I happened to witness what the Sergeant thought to be disrespectful. Honestly, I didn't see it as disrespectful, but then again I was not in his shoes. However, the young Sergeant continued to chew these soldiers up and down until the squad leader, a Staff Sergeant, came over to see what all the commotion was about. The Sergeant told the Staff Sergeant that the troops did not want to follow his orders and that he felt disrespected by all of them. He also said something about setting them all straight, but I was too busy laughing at this point to really catch everything that the Sergeant was saying. The Staff Sergeant asked the soldiers what happened. They explained that the Sergeant wanted all the troops in the tent to go outside and check for trash during their only two-hour break from missions that day. The Staff Sergeant sent the troops back to the tent to rest up for the next mission, and he escorted the young Sergeant away from the area. Only those two know what happened next.

Like I said, I have no clue what was said to the young Sergeant by the Staff Sergeant, but I like to think it went something like this: "Sergeant, you will never really be in charge if you have to tell your guys that you are in charge. They will never respect you if you have to tell them to respect you. These are things you have to earn, and yelling at them because you have three fancy chevrons on your chest isn't going to cut it. Take the time to get to know your soldiers, invest yourself in the areas in which they need improvement, and praise the areas where they excel. All of this will work itself out, and you will earn their respect and trust because that is what we are going to need in a few months when we are in Iraq."

As leaders, we will never be successful leading a team if our team does not have trust, faith, and respect in us. We have to take the advice I am guessing the Staff Sergeant gave the young Sergeant if we want our project or business to be successful. Respect through fear, denigration, and power plays doesn't work. Respect is earned and must be shared by both parties, but it seems that so many people do not understand the value in this, which is truly a shame.

This story also taught me that when you are a leader of managers you cannot address management issues in front of the rest of the team. I have no clue what was really said in that one-on-one conversation because I was only a Private First Class at the time, and if I had heard what was said to the young Sergeant, I would have always doubted that he knew what he was doing. If you have those types of doubts, you will never trust or respect that person. We have to praise our team in public and punish, discipline, or have the tough teaching conversations in private.

Chapter 6
Burnt Out

"The way a team plays as a whole determines its success. You may have the greatest bunch of individual stars in the world, but if they don't play together, the club won't be worth a dime."

— Babe Ruth

In the spring of 2006, our company was preparing to deploy to Iraq. During deployment preparation, everyone is always required to do a lot more work than usual. This extra work is both personal preparation as well as other things that have to be completed at the team, squad, platoon, and company levels. There are so many moving pieces and parts with very limited room for failure. For me and others, it was significantly more stressful getting ready to go on a combat deployment than it was to actually be deployed.

There were so many tasks assigned to our platoon, and our Platoon Sergeant kept assigning our senior Specialist to oversee the majority of these duties because he had been in the United States Army for a few years, and he had a good head on his shoulders. He was arguably our best junior enlisted soldier in our platoon. Because he was such a good soldier, he took on all these additional tasks without complaining about the extra work. He worked many long nights, like we all did at this time. However, when the rest of us went home to our families, he still had other tasks to complete. I am willing to bet his average workday during this time was at least eighteen hours. Working that many hours did not leave much time for him to get his personal affairs in order. Keep in mind that at this time, we thought we were going to be deployed for a year, so there were a lot of items that we had to square away.

All the junior enlisted troops, including myself, could tell that he was stressing out more than an average soldier who was preparing to deploy. I remember talking to some of my buddies about him and our concerns about his stress level, and we didn't even know all the additional tasks that were assigned to him. So we just wrote it off as pre-deployment jitters. If a bunch of young soldiers could pick up on his stress, I am sure the leaders that were tasking him could too— or at least they should have been able to see all of this stress that was building up inside the young Specialist. That did not stop the leadership team from relying on him heavily though, just to get the jobs done.

About a month before we left, I overheard the soldier talking to a group of squad leaders from our platoon. The soldier was voicing his frustration about not being able to get his personal affairs in order and how most nights he didn't even get to see his children because they were already in bed by the time he got home from work. He continued to explain to the squad leaders that the thing that bothered him the most was how unfair it was to his wife, who was basically already a single mother even before he left for a year. He was at his breaking point, and the squad leaders didn't seem to care because nothing changed for this young soldier.

With this high-speed soldier being at his wits' end and with his leadership not seeming to care, he decided to take things into his own hands. He met with some senior leaders from different companies from within our battalion to see who had any openings that he could transfer to and away from the company that had been overworking him. All the senior leaders wanted this very capable soldier, and before too long, several company First Sergeants were fighting to get this soldier on their team and in their company. His transfer paperwork was pushed through the system, and we lost our best junior enlisted troop to a different company in no time at all.

The rumor mill fired up in full force after his transfer was approved. Most guessed that he was simply trying to dodge the deployment, but he had already deployed once and went to a company that was slated to deploy only a few weeks after we were to leave. He clearly wasn't trying to dodge the deployment. Another rumor was that he had a major falling out with the leadership team, but that also wasn't true because the whole leadership team tried to get him to stay. At the end of the day, he was overtasked and not provided the proper resources to balance his work and home lives. It was truly unfortunate for the whole team, squad, platoon, and company not to have a soldier of his caliber deploying with the rest of us.

In today's economy we are all asked to do more work with fewer resources, and in all honesty, that is just good business. However, as leaders we have to be able to balance the demands of the job with being cognizant of our team's workload. If we abuse our go-to person and overtask them, we have to be willing to accept attrition because an overworked employee will end up leaving. We have to have the ability to read people and know when they are reaching their maximum capacity. Most good employees, like a good soldier, will continue to do what is asked of them without bitching or complaining because they do not want to fail their team or project.

It is great to have people like this on our team, but when we put too much on their plate, they end up leaving, with little warning. Once they have made up their mind to leave because they are being overworked, no last-ditch effort to save them will work to keep them on our team. We all know what the financial and workload cost of losing a teammate is, but to lose one of our best has a much larger cost and significantly impacts our team's morale. It is much cheaper for us to step up and actually lead than it is to take a substantial loss like this. By the way, where is the motivation for others on the team if they are never given the opportunity to take on more responsibilities?

Along the same lines, why the hell do we have a team if we are going to task only the top performers? No one who is a true leader likes to get rid of people, but if we have people on our team who cannot do the job, we have to move on and round out our team with people who can balance out the workload and proactively contribute to the mission at hand. The team approach is a very old concept, and one that so many people continue to improperly implement.

At the end of the day, as leaders we have the responsibility to build the best possible team to get a job done. We cannot do that with turnover or underperformers. It is crucial to create a balance of work and life for each individual on the team, and the work needs to be distributed as evenly as possible. This will result in a higher performing, successful team as well as a lower attrition rate.

Chapter 7
Wash Rack in Iraq

"Always do everything you ask of
those your command."

— General George S. Patton

In 2015 a meme was floating around the Internet with a United States Marine holding a mop in his hand and standing outside in a parking lot during a rainstorm. The caption read, "Have you ever fucked up so bad that you had to mop in the rain?" This is a similar story but without the major mistake that leads to mopping in the rain.

The year was either 2006 or 2007 in An Nasiriyah, Iraq. My gun truck team was identified as the most squared-away team the base had to offer; also we were the only team that did not have any favors we could call in to get out of this. So we were assigned the "honor" of showing some General around the base. To this day I cannot remember how many stars this guy had on his collar or what his name was, but he had to be somewhat important with a very impressive title.

It was either December or January, which is why I do not recall the exact year. If you know anything about Iraq, you know that during this time of year, it basically rains nonstop, and the moon dust (the fine, powder-like sand) turns into mud—a type of mud that builds up like concrete and sticks to everything. Should you be able to remove the mud, it still leaves behind an unmistakable brown tint on everything it touched, and I'm not sure that tint ever goes away. Needless to say, our gun truck at this time was a mess inside and out, and that was unacceptable to a man that had spent more than twenty-five years in the United States Army. I learned later in my career that most Generals do not care about little things like a dirty truck in Iraq, but everyone below them seems to think they care and would throw a fit if it was not spotless.

Our gun truck was comprised of a three-man team. We had a Sergeant who was our truck commander, a Specialist, and myself, also a Specialist. The Specialist and I alternated between being the driver and the gunner. We had a HUMVEE with level-five armor and about four miscellaneous antennas mounted to our truck, so it appeared we had the latest and greatest in command and control equipment as well as jammers. Our Sergeant tasked us to make sure the truck was washed and spotless before the next day's mission of showing the General around our little slice of hell. So we loaded up and headed to the wash rack in the rain.

Without any leadership or supervision, we scrubbed the truck for about two hours, but it felt like a lifetime in the cold rain. The outside of the truck looked so good that any soldier would have been proud to roll out of the gate and fight in our truck. However, the inside was still full of moon dust and mud, and it smelled like three grown men had been living out of it for six months in 120-degree heat. We both knew this was unacceptable, and we sprayed out the floors and acquired some unsecured smell-goods from the maintenance shack.

During this process we thought it would be a good idea to cover the driver's seat and the two backseats (for the General and his aide) with plastic trash bags to ensure they stayed dry. We had just enough plastic to cover the makeshift gunner's sling seat because, let's face it, you cannot shoot accurately with wet pants. Unfortunately, we ran out of plastic—or maybe we did not think it would be all that important to cover up our Sergeant's seat because he was not there with us and we were just a little bitter. We called the truck good and made the mile drive back to our living area. When we returned to the living area, the outside of the truck looked the same as it did when we left, but the inside of the truck smelled fantastic.

The next day we picked up the General and his aide at the TOC (tactical operations center) and showed him around our base. We showed the General everything from the gym to the ammunition points where we drew ammunition before every mission. We also took him around to all the TCN (third-country national) restaurants so he could try a few new food items that you could not get in the States. Everything went smoothly except for one little thing—the General wanted to sit in the front seat in order to have a better view. He never once said anything about the wet seat and awarded us a coin for the effort we put into the tour. We also may have given him a tour of our perimeter, which was strictly prohibited for a man of his rank, but I think he enjoyed that part the most.

Believe it or not, I drew several lessons from this experience that have significantly benefited me in the business world. The first was that washing a truck in the rain seemed like a stupid, pointless task, but there was a reason the extra effort was required. The General never once said anything about how the truck looked, but had it looked poor, I am sure someone would have heard about it and it would not have been a pleasant conversation for anyone on our team. In business you always have to put your best foot forward, and that means putting in the extra effort and doing the little things that make you and your team stand out amongst the crowd. Even if the effort seems to go unnoticed, you have to put forth the extra energy because bad impressions are always recognized. Unfortunately, poor impressions stay with the majority of people even more so than good impressions.

The second lesson is along the same lines. Yes, it is the seat. It was funny the first time our Sergeant sat down in the wet seat on our way to go pick up the General and his aide. However, it was not nearly as funny when the General chose to ride in the front seat that was soaking wet. This was the first time I really made the connection that if your leader looks squared away, the whole team looks good. Our leader was walking around with wet pants, and frankly, it was not a good look. Every so often you will find yourself working for someone that you may not like or someone with whom you have some form of a personality or philosophical conflict. You have to rise above that conflict and do everything in your power to make that person look good so that the project, department, or organization is as successful as humanly possible.

I believe the third lesson here is the most obvious, and I think I made that clear in the story with a snide comment about the lack of leadership while we were at the wash rack. Any manager can assign tasks; it really isn't all that difficult to tell people to do something. A true leader steps up and is there for and with his or her employees. We all knew this was an undesirable task that no one wanted to be assigned. In my opinion, the Sergeant should have gone down to the motor pool with us on that rainy day. He did not have to get on the ground, in the mud, to spray down the bottom of the truck because he had put in his time as a junior enlisted soldier, but he should have been present instead of staying back in his hooch (a small two-person trailer used for housing soldiers) playing video games. Had he been down in the motor pool with us, I am certain that his seat would have been covered in plastic and dry like our seats.

This lesson has always stuck with me, especially in the business world. Nine times out of ten I beat my employees into the office, and I am also the one turning off the lights at the end of the workday. A true leader will always present a strong presence to their employees but also give everyone enough space to do their jobs without feeling micromanaged. This is a difficult skill for most people, but if you can perfect this balancing act, I promise you will see happier, more productive employees who experience a higher rate of success.

Chapter 8
Sleeping Pills

*"It all begins with you. If you do
not care for yourself you will not
be strong enough to take care of
anything in life."*

— Leon Brown

In 2007 our mission start times changed a lot while we were deployed. This threw off my internal clock, and I was not able to sleep when I was not out on patrol. Because I was not getting the proper amount of rest, I was constantly exhausted throughout the day. Sitting in the gunner's hatch of a gun truck while you are tasked with protecting your truck and the rest of the trucks out on patrol is not the place to be tired and less than one hundred percent focused because it could cost you your life or worse—the lives of your battle buddies out on the road with you.

For several days I experimented with multiple ways to get some rest. I tried working out before I lay down to sleep, going on a run then trying to sleep, and taking a lot of short naps. None of these helped me get the rest I needed to perform at my best on our missions. I finally gave up and decided to go see the doctor to get some assistance with my sleeping issues in the form of sleeping pills.

The appointment with the doctor was very similar to a mental-health evaluation. The doctor wanted to make sure that my schedule was what was throwing off my sleep and that I was not struggling with combat stress. I would like to say it was just my schedule, but I am sure leaving the security of our base every night looking for IEDs (improvised explosive devices or roadside bombs) could have also played into my lack of quality sleep. For the most part though, it was just my schedule and not the combat that was causing me not to sleep and not to be able recharge for the next mission.

After the evaluation, the doctor prescribed me a very common sleeping drug. I waited a day before taking the pills because I was off work the following day. I wanted to make sure I was off work the first time I took the medicine in case any of the many side effects affected me. I am not a huge fan of taking medicine; in fact, to this day I will rarely take any type of medicine, including over-the-counter pain medicine, even for a headache that will not go away.

I took the prescribed number of pills at 0900 (9:00 a.m.) because my new schedule had me working all night. I walked the 150 yards to the restrooms and back. In that short amount of time, I was already beginning to feel a little bit loopy. I figured the drug was doing its thing, so I crawled into bed. At this time I was living in a very small two-person trailer, and our mini refrigerator was located directly across from my bed.

About thirty minutes after I lay down, my refrigerator opened then closed all on its own. Then it scooted closer to my bed and opened and closed again. I truly felt like my life was going to end and that my refrigerator was going to eat me. I quickly grabbed my rifle and put three rounds into my refrigerator and fell fast asleep for about nine hours or so. (We lived close to the test firing pit, so no one thought twice about hearing shots fired.)

After I woke up, I saw that my floor was soaked from the busted water bottles and that my refrigerator was destroyed. I immediately got dressed and took the pills back to the hospital and refused to ever take them again. I also went to the Post Exchange to buy a new refrigerator before my roommate returned from his day mission—or more shots could have been fired.

Once again, this is an extreme case, but this story still provides valuable lessons. The first is if you are going to put anything into your body for the first time, make sure you are in a safe environment. I think I will just leave that one at that.

The second lesson is that as leaders we have to take care of ourselves if we are going to take care of others. This is different for all of us. I personally function best with six to eight hours of sleep. You might need more or less, but we all need rest to recharge our batteries. If we are not able to give one hundred percent of our attention and focus to the task at hand, how can we ever expect others to give us their all?

I know that potentially falling asleep in the gunner's hatch with a .50-caliber machine gun in front of you would not commonly happen to most of us. But think about what could go wrong in your average day if you are not fully engaged. Could you misread some numbers in a report and make a poor decision? Could you misunderstand the details of a deal you are about to make? Could you be snippy and rude to the wrong person? Or could you lack enough energy to properly help one of your employees with an issue that they were experiencing? All of these are bad and could create a lot of problems for you down the road if they were to happen. It is obvious that taking care of ourselves, body and mind, is a priority. It would be quite difficult to take care of the people around us and the business at hand if we were not in the correct condition ourselves.

Sleep is only one aspect of taking care of ourselves; taking care of ourselves goes a lot deeper than sleep. We have to make sure that we do not let health issues go unresolved because, as you can see, they could impact every phase of business. Every aspect of our health is important if we want to be successful. We have to take care of our mental, physical, and spiritual health if we want to reach our full potential, and if we want to be able to give the people around us the best support and leadership we have to offer.

Chapter 9
Perception

"The perception of the audience is the interesting part. If the audience doesn't hear what is going on, is it going on or not?"

— Robert Fripp

In the spring of 2007, I was still assigned as a gunner and driver on a gun truck that was assigned to protect our fairly large Air Base in Iraq. It was a great assignment, and I loved that it kept us on our toes and moving every night. We would spend our twelve-hour shifts driving up and down the major highway that ran north and south right outside our base looking for IEDs (improvised explosive devices or road side bombs). We had a great team of guys, and we were constantly joking around; there was never a shortage of laughter or pranks. We also had a good Platoon Sergeant, but he could never seem to get along with our senior leadership. This created some waves for us; he always had our backs though, so we would have followed him anywhere.

One night we were at the TOC all loaded up to roll out on our patrol mission when we were notified that our mission had changed. We were no longer going to go driving around looking for IEDs; instead, we were going to go sit outside our base's burn pit to be a show of force to the locals that were breaking into the burn pit to steal scrap metal to sell. Don't get me wrong, this was an issue because scrap metal was being used to make IEDs at this time. But honestly, who really wants to sit by a burn pit the size of two football fields for twelve hours a day? To top it all off, it just smelled terrible.

The TOC told us that the whole team was under investigation, but they never provided any further details. The investigation went on for several weeks or a month, and we continued to guard the burn pit. We were finally able to return to the road, and the only thing that changed was that we had a new Platoon Sergeant. To this day I still have no clue what they actually investigated, but in the end, the senior leadership got what they wanted and our Platoon Sergeant was replaced.

Who knows what the senior leadership perceived to be the issue with our team or what the problems were with our Platoon Sergeant. But the age-old adage is true here: perception is reality, and our senior leadership thought they had to do something. The reason I say "perception is reality" is that none of our senior leadership ever left the base with us. They had no clue what we were doing outside the wire or what we did on a mission. The same was true in reverse. We had no clue what went on in the TOC or what our senior leadership did during the day. Our perception was that all they did was drink coffee, eat donuts, and tell us what to check out while we were out on the road. Our perception was based on the little things we heard from our Platoon Sergeant, and they were never very nice. Right, wrong, or indifferent, these were the perceptions that became both sides' realities.

Now that I am a little further along in my career and have been in similar leadership positions, like the Platoon Sergeant, I know that as leaders we are responsible for creating the perception of our team. Most of the time, when we speak, people will listen to what we have to say. Not only are they listening to our words, but they are also paying attention to how we say things and to our body language. The Platoon Sergeant could have easily given us a different reality of what was going on behind the scenes in the TOC by delivering the messages differently.

Although we would have followed our Platoon Sergeant anywhere, it took us all a long time to warm up to our new Platoon Sergeant because of what we thought we knew about the senior leadership and who they selected to run our team. When these relationships take time to develop, we lose productivity and are prone to accidents due to the lack of trust. This is never beneficial to any organization.

Chapter 10
Ottie

*"I truly believe if you take care of
your employees, they will take care
of your business."*

— Richard Branson

In 2007 our government decided to do a surge in Iraq to regain some ground they perceived we had lost. In order to gain the additional troops needed on the ground in Iraq, the Department of Defense sent replacements on the usual timeline, but they extended the troops that were already in Iraq for an additional three months. You guessed it: I was already on the ground and got extended for three months.

The usual United States Army deployment at this time was twelve months. My unit was scheduled to redeploy back to the States in early August after the twelve months we spent in Iraq, but our new date was early October. However, when we got the extension notice, we had already turned over our mission to our replacements. We didn't really have anything to do besides hit the gym, cause trouble in the MWR (Moral Welfare and Recreation Center where we could call home and access the Internet) and DFAC, and play cards in our tents.

We also had to vacate our nice, enclosed, air-conditioned hooches and move into a tent city in the 120-degree Iraqi heat. I would be lying if I said anything about our living conditions besides they absolutely sucked. If you ask me, the worst thing in the military is a bored soldier. You never know what type of trouble they will find, and you better believe that they will find it. My battle buddies and I were no exceptions to this, and we found a lot of trouble during our stay in tent city. Also during this time my beloved grandmother was dying of a very sudden illness back in Evansville, Indiana. A bored soldier with personal issues back home is a recipe for disaster.

I never had any luck getting emergency leave approved during my time in the military, and this was my first experience trying to request this type of leave. In mid-August I received a Red Cross letter stating that my grandmother was in the ICU, and the chances for recovery were not looking good. I already knew this information because my family was keeping me informed, but in the United States Army a soldier cannot be trusted to pass along information like this. All notifications have to be formal and go through the Red Cross. It is used as a verification process because, believe it or not, some people like to abuse the system. (I mostly blame Corporal Klinger, from *M*A*S*H*, for this.)

Once I was formally notified, I immediately started the process to go home on emergency leave to be with my family during this difficult time. I thought surely the company could give me up for two weeks because all I was doing was causing trouble around the base with the rest of my bored battle buddies. I was wrong and devastated to hear that my request for emergency leave was denied.

I know this may sound silly to some to get this worked up about a grandparent, but I was very close with all my grandparents. All four of my grandparents lived in the same town in Indiana. My brother, sister, and I would spend our summers down in Indiana bouncing back and forth between our grandparents' houses as well as hanging out with our cousins. Those summers and all those memories will always be part of who I am. Being so far away from home while losing my third grandparent was extremely painful for me.

A few more days went by, again with me doing nothing but playing cards, hitting the gym, and generally goofing off. So I figured I would request a Red Cross update on my grandmother from my family. My family sent one, this time saying it was only a matter of time; there was no chance of recovery. I already knew this because we had an amazing ICU nurse who was keeping me informed via email, but unless the Red Cross sends a letter, it is like it never happened. Now that I was armed with a nice paper trail, I submitted another leave packet. I ended up with the same disappointing results as last time, DENIED!

In the middle of the night on August 25, 2007, in Iraq, and in the late afternoon on August 24th back in the States, my grandmother passed away. My family, who was well educated on the Red Cross process by now, sent a third Red Cross letter. My company Commander, a Captain, walked into my tent, kicked my cot, dropped the Red Cross letter on my chest, and said, "Your grandmother has passed away." Then the Captain walked out of my tent without saying another word.

I jumped out of my cot and ran out of my tent, chasing the Captain and wearing nothing but socks, boxers, and a tan T-shirt. I remember saying, "Now will you fucking send me home?" (He remembered me saying something that was a lot worse and even more disrespectful. What I actually said was probably somewhere in between what we both remembered.) The Captain told me no, and there was a little bit of a physical altercation. This probably set my career back a few years, but rumor has it that due to the Captain's lack of leadership throughout our entire deployment, he was forced out of the United States Army. However, he was honest because he did in fact deny my third and final attempt to go home on emergency leave.

The Captain did get two more punches in after we got back to the States and before he disappeared from our company. The first was a smart comment he made to me when we got off the bus back at Fort Lee about how he would now approve my leave request. (It was too late then because my grandmother was already buried, and my family had a few days to process everything at this time.) He also made sure that I was the very last soldier to walk into the field house to meet our families after fourteen months down range. Two points to the Captain, but I still had a promising military career ahead of me.

First, let's address what I think is the most obvious lesson in this story and that is poor leadership or the lack of leadership in general. This whole book is designed for people who want to be better leaders, and oddly enough, I have learned more from poor leaders than I have from some of the best leaders I have had the privilege to serve under. I believe this is because bad impressions stay with people.

The Captain had the authority to approve my emergency leave request. It was not going to cost him anything or create any additional work for anyone because all our equipment and gear were already packed and cleared by United States Customs. We couldn't touch the stuff even if we wanted to. There were multiple flights a day heading back to the States, again with no additional costs to the unit. He also would not have lost any political gains in the process, and I would argue that he would have actually gained some political points with his troops by supporting my leave request. So whenever you can help someone and it doesn't show favoritism or cause any additional work for the rest of team, always do what you can to support and help the person. Although this is not a very difficult concept to grasp, most seem to forget what we were all taught at a young age—the Golden Rule. "Do unto others as you would have others do unto you."

Let's go back to the physical altercation that occurred. Physical altercations are never the best way to handle any situation, but thankfully we do not see that all that often in business or in the office. The second part of the lesson here was that the physical altercation in the story was based entirely on emotion. Whenever you react based off emotion, you are not making a decision. It is not always easy to remove emotion from the decision-making process, but as a leader you have to do your best to remove as much emotion as possible to make the best fact-based decision. This is not easy, and at times it can delay a decision as you take the step back and process all the available information. However, if you do this, you will achieve a better decision that will lead to more rewarding results.

Chapter 11
Formation

"Nothing replaces being in the same room, face-to-face, breathing the same air and reading and feeling each other's micro-expressions."

— Peter Gruber

In 2007 after our deployment, our new leadership, the First Sergeant in particular, decided to start holding a formation every working day at 1630 (4:30 p.m.). A formation is when the whole company comes together in three or four lines, depending on how the platoons are structured, with about ten feet separating each platoon. Whoever calls the formation is out front and center and should have everyone's undivided attention.

Most days, the First Sergeant would walk out of his office and release us for the night because he didn't have any new information to pass along to the rest of the company. Other days, he would push out new information that came down from our battalion or some new regulation that came from the Department of Defense. He would also use this formation to publicly recognize soldiers, a squad, or platoon that did a good job or went above and beyond to make the whole company look good. These were always upbeat formations and usually led to a day off for the guys getting recognized. However, there were also less positive formations when the First Sergeant had to explain what some soldier did that got them into trouble. No matter what the situation was, all of these formations were usually short and lasted only about ten minutes or so from start to finish.

At this time I was a young Specialist, and I did not see the value in holding these formations at the end of every day. Like I said, most days there was no new information provided to us. I also remember thinking to myself that, when information was provided, a simple email to the Platoon Sergeant would have sufficed to get the information to the people who actually needed to know what was going on. As a Specialist I didn't need to know much besides the task at hand and where the nearest Private was to do the worst part of the task.

As the years have gone by, I like to think that I have grown, learned, and matured from the time that I wore the shame shield of the Specialist. I also have to admit that I have changed my views on the formations that the First Sergeant called. There is something to be said for face-to-face interaction on a regular basis with the people who work for or with you.

Texting, email, and phone calls are great tools for saving time and energy, but they are certainly not replacements for personal interactions and communication. Have you ever looked at someone and sensed that they were stressed out about something or having a bad day? Of course, we all have. It is vital to have the personal interaction, or else it would be impossible to pick up on these types of signs and signals. I am not suggesting that you stop using the tools at your disposal to be more efficient with your time. All I am saying is that as leaders we have a personal responsibility to ensure that we do not become disconnected from our teams by hiding behind our tools. We have to maintain a certain level of personal interaction with every member of our team so that we can be proactive in correcting something that may not have worked out quite right for someone. This is one of the major differences between a good leader and great one.

Chapter 12
DUI Night

"The two words 'information' and 'communication' are often used interchangeably, but they signify quite different things. Information is giving out; communication is getting through."

— Sydney J. Harris

On a beautiful November night, shortly after my twenty-first birthday, I was enjoying dinner with my roommate at our favorite national chain restaurant and bar. During dinner we were chatting about our recent deployment and how we spent our block leave after the deployment, as well as what we wanted to do and had to do that coming weekend. We were just getting back in the swing of normal military life in the States. It was just two buddies having a typical dinner.

Shortly after finishing our meals and our second or third beer (depends on who is telling the story), I got a call from one of my soldiers. He informed me that he had been arrested by the MPs (military police) for driving under the influence of alcohol. This is going to sound very bad, but we pretty much expected this to happen to at least one young soldier after a deployment. When a soldier had been deployed with very little freedom, in a country with hundreds of thousand—if not millions—of people who were trying to kill them for the last year, they tended to forget their limits and embraced the freedoms they had been fighting for. Also, getting busted by the military police is not the same as getting busted by the "real" police. At this time, all it took was a senior NCO or officer to come down to the jail and sign you out. Then your punishment would come down in the form of an Article 15, or non-judicial punishment.

We finished up our conversation, and I headed back to the base to meet up with the rest of the leadership team to sign my soldier out of jail. At this time I did not have enough rank to sign him out myself, but I wanted to make sure the senior leaders understood that I was dedicated to the success of my soldiers and that I was taking responsibility for their actions. One minor fact that my soldier forgot to mention to me was that he got busted at a 100 percent breathalyzer checkpoint on base at the only gate that was open at that time of night. This is where a military police officer would conduct a breathalyzer test on every driver entering the base, without any probable cause. This was a very crucial piece of information that would have been good to know.

I got stopped just like everyone else trying to enter the gate of our base, and I had to blow into a breathalyzer. I was not drunk by any means, but apparently my breath was drunk enough to blow exactly the legal limit of .08. Right or wrong, I ended up getting to the jail via a complimentary ride in a police car. Before being processed, I got the chance to use my cell phone to notify my leadership that we had a slightly larger issue than just my soldier being locked up. My boss, who was a Staff Sergeant, said only, "See you when you get here," and he hung up. What I did not know at that time was that he meant, "Cool. When you get here, we will share a cell." (I am not trying to make light of drinking and driving because it is a real issue that needs to be curbed.)

All the arrests that night could have been prevented. First, everyone involved could and should have taken a step back and thought to themselves, "Hey, dumbass, you have been drinking. Do not get behind the wheel of a car." How many times have you made a rash business decision as a leader that had unintentional consequences? We all have. The key here is to take the time and think through what you are doing. This is a concept that we all have to implement every day, and it takes some personal restraint not to jump to conclusions. If you rush to judgment and pull the trigger early, it can come back to bite you in the ass or, depending on how bad the situation is, could land you in jail. I know that is the extreme, but the story I just told shows that it is most certainly possible.

Second, this could have been prevented with communication. I will focus on my failure in this situation first. I did not ask any questions as to how my soldier got arrested. My soldier just told me that he got arrested, I cussed, and then I told him I would be there in a little while to pick him up. I let the frustration of the situation get to me, and it never crossed my mind to ask for the facts. Had I known the facts, I would have never driven on base that night. Now, as a business leader and more of an adult, I know things are going to go wrong from time to time, and I react differently, except for the cussing part. That seems to still be my natural reaction when things go wrong. Now when bad news is broken to me, the first thing I do is ask the "why questions." The why questions are: Why did this happen? How could've we prevented this? What is the best path forward, from your point of view? How do we prevent this from happening again? Once the facts are presented, as a team or by ourselves (depending on the situation), we can come up with a well-thought-out recovery plan, instead of a reaction plan based off emotion or a lack of information.

Now, on to the soldier's failure that night. Besides the fact that he got himself locked up, he never provided the facts or a solution. Instead of just saying he got arrested for DUI, he could have explained the situation regarding his arrest. He should have said, "Hey, I got arrested at a 100 percent checkpoint at the main gate for DUI." With just a little more information like this, we would have made a better decision, and the information could have been socialized throughout the team, peers, and superiors. Whenever we elevate a problem, we need to be able to provide a solution to the issue at hand.

In the world we live in today, information is king. The more information we have, the better off any project will be. The same is true in reverse. The less information we have, the less likely it is the project will be successful. Information is passed via communication from one person to another. It is just as important to be an effective communicator to ensure that our critical information is passed on effectively. In business we have to arm ourselves with the very best information we can get our hands on to protect and advance our projects.

Chapter 13
The Move

"A good plan violently executed now is better than a perfect plan executed next week."

— George S. Patton

Back in 2007 I was stationed in Virginia but had orders to move to Kentucky. On my last deployment I had reenlisted for this move in order to be closer to family who lived in Ohio and Indiana. My orders stated that I was to report to Fort Knox no later than 10 January 2008. However, because I was single, trying to escape a bad personal relationship, and trying to move closer to family after a deployment, I chose to report early and left Virginia near the end of November or early December.

As a junior enlisted soldier you cannot PCS (permanent change of station) without a major blowout party with all your friends from the base you are departing. So the night before I was going to make the ten-hour drive to Kentucky, my fellow soldiers kidnapped me, and we had one last night out on the town in Richmond, Virginia. The night was a blast. We hung out at a very laid-back bar and swapped stories from our deployment and the other shenanigans we pulled in the motor pool and around the barracks. The turnout was great, and everyone that I cared about from the area was present.

It was such a blast that I totally forgot to load up the U-Haul trailer that I rented to move all my personal belongings that night. (Just so you know, my personal belongings consisted of one La-Z-Boy recliner; three or four tough boxes of military gear; five or six duffel bags of civilian clothes; and one fairly large box of military paperwork, awards, coins, and so on. I did not have a whole lot back then—a total value of maybe a couple grand.)

The morning following my going-away party, my roommate and I rushed to carry all my personal belongings down from our third-floor barracks room to the U-Haul trailer. We finished with about thirty seconds to spare before the barracks NCOIC showed up to inspect my room. His signature was the second-to-last signature I needed before I could start my journey. During the inspection he did a quick once-over of my room and checked my refrigerator. Then he asked if I planned on taking the four or five beers that were still in there. I said no; he took the beers and signed my papers.

After losing my beer, I headed over to our Group Headquarters to sign out on leave. The last signature I needed was my own. I was finally free for a few days before I had to report to my new base in Kentucky. I hit the road, heading west back toward my home state of Ohio to spend a few days with my family.

My drive started with a quick pit stop at a truck stop to get my vehicle weighed and to pick up some beef jerky and sweet tea for the drive. On a side note, when you move yourself, the Army reimburses you based on the weight of the items you move, which is why I stopped at the weigh station. I guess that was really when I felt that sense of freedom. I enjoyed my time at Fort Lee, but I was more than happy to be heading west for a new adventure.

The drive was beautiful. It was a sunny, early winter day, and I was driving with the music turned up to drown out my terrible singing. I made it about fifty miles or so down Interstate 64 before my trailer made a God-awful noise. The trailer was swaying back and forth, damn near across all three lanes. Luckily there was little to no traffic that day. I slowed down and got to the right-hand shoulder of the highway. After catching my breath and regaining my composure, I finally got the nerve to go take a look to see what happened. It turned out that the ball on my trailer hitch was still connected to the trailer, but the nut that held the ball to the hitch was missing. I laughed a little bit and decided that the best thing to do would be to leave the trailer and head into town to buy a new hitch. I unhooked the towing chains and drove off in my Expedition in search of a hardware store.

It would have been convenient to have a smart phone back then because it took me thirty minutes to find a Lowes Home Improvement store to buy a new hitch. Then it also would have been nice to drop a pin where I left the trailer because I spent an hour looking for it before I gave up. Eventually I realized that the U-Haul was gone and called the Virginia Highway Patrol to report the trailer stolen.

Once the highway patrol officer showed up, I told him what happened, and he asked me to follow him back to his station so that he could take my written statement and fill out a report. So much for that freedom that I thought I had. Once at the state patrol office, I gave my statement and contact information to his boss and was told that they would be in contact should they find the trailer. I had never been so happy in my life that I spent the extra few dollars on insurance with U-Haul.

So that I don't leave you hanging, the local news station ran the story on Crime Stoppers, and the trailer was recovered about a month later. All that was left inside the trailer was a stick of deodorant. To my knowledge, no arrests were ever made. I would also like to take a moment to thank the woman from the area who took up a collection at her church and sent me a check to help out with the loss. The biggest thing that was lost that day was not my clothes or recliner, but my whole military career was documented in that box of paperwork.

To this day I am still shocked that all of this happened, but I definitely learned from it, and I am sure that is the real reason I had this experience. Like

I said, the biggest thing I lost was a couple boxes of paperwork. At the time, I was most upset that I lost all my awards because awards in the United States Army are worth promotion points, and I needed all the points I could get to help me make Sergeant. It wasn't until about eight years after this happened that I was reminded by a very smart woman that it was not about the fancy paper that made the award; it was about the experiences that led to the award. Those experiences were the real takeaway. After those kind words, she then she called me a dumbass for not updating my official files with the awards. So the other takeaway is to make sure you keep up with your official records, whether they are military records, human resources records, resumes, or any other type of documentation you may have in your life.

I had a plan for this move. I rented the trailer, and I had all my paperwork in order. Aside from my barracks room being cleared, I had all my out-processing completed in a timely manner. But hey, I had to have a place to sleep. What I did not do was execute on my plans. I should have inspected the hitch, and I also should have packed the night before. Honestly, I do not think it would have made a difference had I loaded up the trailer and pushed the start time for my going-away party thirty minutes or so. Let's face it, all I really needed was a set of clean clothes and some toiletries the morning of the move, and all of those would have been just fine in the passenger seat of my truck.

As a leader you can have some of the best-made plans in the world for your project or business, but if you are not prepared to execute, you are more than likely to fail. I have never met a leader who wants to fail.

Chapter 14
The Board

"Success is where preparation and opportunity meet."

— Bobby Unser

In 2008 a battle buddy of mine and I were selected to attend the Sergeant promotion board. This was a big deal for us as Specialists because it meant that our leadership team thought that we were ready to pin on the rank of Sergeant and officially lead soldiers. In the United States Army you must have a certain number of years of service as well as so many years in your current rank (known as time in grade) to be considered for the promotion board. Even though you must meet these two criteria, not everyone gets the privilege to attend the promotion board when they hit these milestones. You have to be nominated by your squad and Platoon Sergeant. After that you will be interviewed by your

First Sergeant and Company Commander, all of these interviews need to have favorable outcomes. Then you also have to do a massive stack of paperwork and make sure all your records are up-to-date.

Soon after my battle buddy and I passed all of these steps with flying colors, we began learning and memorizing the Non-Commissioned Officer's Creed, a three-paragraph creed that to this day I still use to help define myself as a leader. The other NCOs in the company were encouraged to ask all the soldiers going to the promotion board to recite the NCO Creed whenever they saw us. Heaven forbid we should screw up reciting their creed. They would force us to do something, usually push-ups, to ensure it did not happen again. The NCOs were also highly encouraged to ask us board questions throughout the day as well. Again, wrong answers resulted in push-ups. Because of my hatred toward push-ups, I spent my nights studying for the board after work. I also had two Sergeants in particular who took me under their wings and studied with me throughout the day at work, lunch, and any other time we could fit it in. I remember one of them asking board questions at softball practice. That goes to show how badly they all wanted to see us succeed. By the end of these several weeks, both my battle buddy and I thought our heads were going to explode.

Our big day finally came, and my battle buddy and I reported to our battalion headquarters at 0830 (8:30 a.m.) for the board that started at 0930 (9:30 a.m.). Our sponsor, who was a Staff Sergeant, met us there early to do a double-check on our dress uniforms. He ensured that everything was spaced and properly in line. I think dress uniforms look great on soldiers, and it is their time to show off what they have accomplished, but damn are they a pain to put together correctly. We stood around for a while because we were too afraid to sit down and wrinkle our uniforms. Needless to say, we were very nervous, but we tried to keep our nervousness to ourselves and not let anyone see us shaking.

Having the last name of Ripplinger put me toward the back of the pack to actually enter the board room because the board was conducted in alphabetic order. I was left in a waiting room right outside the board room with all the other soldiers and NCOs that were attending the boards that day. Some would walk into the board and right back out for failing to do something correctly. Unfortunately, those people had to wait another month to try it again. Others would be in the board room for ten to fifteen minutes while others spent about half an hour with the board. There was no telling what all this meant because we would not get the results until later in the day. My battle buddy went three people before me and spent about twenty minutes with the board. When he walked out, he shook his hand side to side to signal he had no clue how he did. I should also add that we were not supposed to talk to one another in the waiting room. We were only allowed to talk to our sponsor, and even that was kept to a minimum.

In no time flat, I was up. I knocked three times, entered the board room, and presented myself to the president of the board. The president of the board was our Battalion Command Sergeant Major. He had two First Sergeants on each side of him that made up the board. The four First Sergeants were the ones to assign a score from 0 to 150 based on our performance. Then they would average the four scores to make up our final score, and that's how many promotion points we would receive from the board. The Command Sergeant Major was there to guide the First Sergeants and had no official say in our scores, but he was the one who would throw soldiers out of the board for failing to do something correctly.

After I presented myself to the board, the Command Sergeant Major asked me to turn around to make sure my uniform was properly tailored to my body. He asked me to recite the Soldiers Creed and the Creed of the Non-Commissioned Officer. I sounded off as loud as I could and did not miss a word of either. I was feeling very confident at this time. The Command Sergeant Major then yielded the floor to the first First Sergeant, who asked me three questions on Army regulations, technical manuals, and field manuals. I nailed the first three questions. Then he asked me to tell him the field manual that covered land navigation. I responded with field manual 3-26.56, which was incorrect and I knew it right away because the correct field manual was 3-25.26. This was when my nerves kicked in again.

The next two First Sergeants asked their questions, and I did fine with those. I am not sure how many I missed, but I responded with confidence and my answers sounded correct even if they were not. The last First Sergeant asked about current events, such as what was going on in Libya and who won the football games on Sunday. Luckily I love football, and I have always followed the news; I was able to answer his questions fairly easily as well. The Command Sergeant Major then asked if I wanted to change any of my answers or wanted to add any other statements for the board to consider. I politely thanked the board for their time and consideration, saluted, and exited the board room.

I felt the same way as my battle buddy after the board; I had no clue how I did overall. Once we were released from the board, my battle buddy and I figured we would change out of our dress uniforms and head off base for lunch. We were both hoping a couple burgers would help ease our excitement while we waited for the call that our results were in. We tried to make small talk, but it was very clear that we only had our results on our minds.

We finally got the call as we walked to our vehicles, but they wouldn't give us the results over the phone. We both rushed back to our company headquarters to find out our scores and sign our last piece of paperwork, which was our promotion point validation form. My battle buddy beat me to the company and was already with the personnel specialist when I arrived. When he finished doing his paperwork, he came out with his head down and stated that he wasn't happy with his score as he walked straight past me and headed to his car. Once again I became nervous as I walked in to get my results. I scored a 149.75 and lost one point from the land navigation First Sergeant. The rest of the First Sergeants gave me 150s, but the United States Army rounds down in these situations. Overall I had 650-some-odd total promotion points, (after they included the additional points I earned though weapons qualification, physical training, education, and awards) enough to almost guarantee making the Sergeants' list the following month. My battle buddy scored a 138 on the board, if I am not mistaken, and only had a total in the low 500s.

My battle buddy studied his ass off for the next month, and we all pitched in to help him where we could. I can only imagine how many hours he spent studying that month. He scored a 150 on the next month's board and was recommended for the Soldier of the Month board the following month. He did everything he had to do to get his total points up and pinned on Sergeant a month or two after I did. He was an inspiration to the rest of the soldiers in our platoon.

The first takeaway I had from this experience was something that I rarely see in corporate America— cooperation. All the Sergeants in our company could have very easily told us to study on our own. Some did, but the majority of the Sergeants stepped up and helped us by passing on their knowledge. They didn't have to take us to lunch or pull us aside to teach us what was required to have a successful board appearance. They did all of this because they wanted to help the young guys out. They saw the value in working together to help someone by bringing us up to their level instead of holding us back to make themselves look better.

I believe this mindset in corporations would improve the workforce and lead to a larger share of the market because this type of positive attitude is contagious. When you have a very positive, cooperative attitude and culture, suppliers want to provide the same level of service to you. Customers will want to do more business with a company with this strong attitude toward joint success. So much of business is based off relationships, and for the life of me, I cannot understand why so many companies do not employ this methodology. Sticking with the outdated, cut-throat, competitive attitude will get us only outdated results.

The second lesson I learned from this story was that we have to conduct ourselves in a way that projects confidence. I am sure I answered more questions incorrectly than just the land navigation question, but I gave my answers with confidence, and the First Sergeants never questioned my answers. I am not saying it is right to give the wrong answer as long as we are confident. What I am getting at here is that as leaders, we have to do everything in our power to have all the facts and pertinent information to make the correct decision, and when we reach the best possible answer or solution, we have to deliver the message with confidence. This creates excitement and leaves no doubts in the minds of the people receiving the message. No one is going to fully follow a leader who cannot deliver a clear, concise, confident message.

The third and final takeaway from this story comes from my battle buddy. We all get knocked down or have things not go our way from time to time, but it is how we react to these situations that set the average apart from the great. My battle buddy probably had a very rough night the night after the board, and I am sure he beat himself up pretty bad as well. However, the next day he got up and hit the books with a plan to attend the next board. He did not sit around feeling sorry for himself, and he did not do all of this on his own. He asked for help from all of us. We ran several mock boards to help him prepare for the next board and to help build up his confidence in himself after the last official board. He sought out the help that he needed to get him to where he wanted to be, but he also did what he had to do to get ready for the next opportunity.

As leaders we have to know when we need to ask for help, and we have to do everything we can to get our team to where we want it to be. A joint effort with the right people will always be more beneficial to the team than if you are too stubborn and try to do everything yourself.

Chapter 15
Waiver to Deploy

*"Ten soldiers wisely led will beat a
hundred without a head."*

— Euripides

Back sometime around 2007 or 2008, the Army started to realize that they were deploying the same soldiers over and over again. I have my own theory on why this was happening, but that is an entirely different story for a different day. I was deployed from 2006 to 2007 for a little over fourteen months. While deployed, I reenlisted and chose to move to a base in Kentucky to be closer to family. The day I in-processed my new duty station, I was notified that I would be going back to Iraq in just a few months. At this time I had not yet met my wife, and I did not have kids, so it was no big deal for me to go back to Iraq, although my mother would probably argue that point.

As soon as I finished the very lengthy in-processing, all I wanted to do was meet my soldiers and assess their readiness to deploy. I could then begin building a training program so that we all could have a successful deployment and, most importantly, so that we all could come home safe and sound. (Side note: To this day, bringing all my troops and battle buddies home from combat is the best achievement of my professional career and always will be.) As the time got closer to our deployment date, I was notified that I would not be able to deploy with my guys because I did not have enough of this new thing called "dwell time," which is the United States Army's way of ensuring that every soldier had an equal amount of time home as they did deployed. For example, if a soldier was deployed for twelve months, he or she had to be back at his or her home base for twelve months before deploying again.

I think you all know enough about me and the way I think and feel by now to know I was not going to let that fly without a fight. I was not going to train my guys to deploy and then say to them, "See you all in a few months once I hit this dwell time thing." So I did some research and found out it is not really all that difficult to waive your dwell time. You just need a One Star General (or higher) to sign your waiver, and you need to pass a mental-health exam.

The next day, I went to the mental-health clinic and scheduled an exam, which I passed. Wonder what every major military base has on it? Yes, a One Star or better. So I called up the General's office, and his very rude secretary informed me that some Sergeant cannot just call up the General. I was aware of this, but I clearly stated on my phone call that I needed a favor from the secretary. Some people just won't lend a helping hand, and there is nothing you can do about that. But wait—it gets worse. The secretary felt it was her job to call my battalion and snitch on me. I have no problems reporting people for not doing the right thing, but seriously, lady, I was trying to go down range with the soldiers I was responsible for. You could have told me his tee time or some other way to make this happen.

Now I get called to the Battalion Command Sergeant Major's office, which was becoming a familiar place for me and not in a good way. Much like every other visit to the Command Sergeant Major's office, it started with a well-deserved ass-chewing. However, the Command Sergeant Major asked me why I thought I needed to see the General. I filled him in on my dwell time issue and that I was not going to send my guys down range without me. Dwell time was new to him as well. Thankfully, this crusty old Command Sergeant Major had an old-school sense of leadership and agreed with what I was trying to accomplish. Then he remembered how I went about it, and that was round two of the same ass-chewing. However, the Command Sergeant Major arranged for me to meet with the Battalion Commander (Lieutenant Colonel). The Battalion Commander was also an old crusty leader and understood where I was coming from and said he would see what he could do.

A few days later, the Command Sergeant Major called me something that I probably shouldn't repeat in this book, but he also informed me that my waiver to deploy was approved. I went back home to Ohio that weekend to let my family know in person that I was heading back to Iraq. During that trip back home, I met a very special girl who ultimately became my wife. Although leaving her made my deployment much more difficult, I would still make the same decision to waive my dwell time ten times out of ten.

There comes a time in all our careers that we have to step up and make personal sacrifices for the greater good—that could be our people, our projects, our company, or even our country. Had I waited for my dwell time to pass, it would not have changed the outcome of the war by any means, but it could have changed the outcome of the deployment for my troops. There were plenty of other good leaders I worked with that deployment that would have taken care of them, but it wouldn't have been the same. I do believe that every one of my soldiers worked a little harder that deployment because they had faith in their whole leadership team. I was not the only leader in the chain of command to waive their dwell time. During that deployment, we set the standard for success as a platoon. I firmly believe this was because of the sacrifices all of us leaders made.

Giving up three or four months of your life to go fight in Iraq when you did not have to is an extreme example of sacrifice. As a business leader, it is very important to be a strong leader who is willing to make sacrifices to earn the respect and trust of your people.

Chapter 16
Washing Windows

"The first responsibility of a leader is to define reality. The last is to say thank you. In between, the leader is a servant."

— Max de Pree

As a new leader in an organization, you have to do things to gain the trust among your colleagues. This story is my version of gaining my troops' trust, but it ended up causing me a lot more work.

I was a newly promoted Sergeant—I am not even sure if the ink was dry on my promotion orders. It was late May in 2008, and we were slated to deploy again in early August. During this time of the deployment rotation, if we were not training, we were spending as much time with our friends and family as possible.

On this day in late May, we were all smokin' and jokin' at the motor pool. The First Sergeant requested or, more accurately, demanded that the motor pool be cleaned and all the trucks be on line. On line is just a fancy way of saying that all the trucks are parked in a line and flush with one another. This is a normal task—a very annoying but common task. Our motor pool was located in a valley with a gravel parking lot for our personal cars located above the motor pool.

At 1500 (3:00 p.m.) we already had the motor pool clean, and the trucks were all on line. I thought it was a good idea to send my troops home. The usual go-home time was 1700 (5:00 p.m.) on a good day, but they all worked hard, and in my opinion, the motor pool looked great. I didn't like to keep people at work for no reason, and I thought sending everyone home a couple hours early would help gain their trust and respect prior to the upcoming deployment. I stuck around for about another forty-five minutes or so finishing up paperwork.

On my way to my personal truck to go spend the weekend with a new fling, who turned out not to be just a fling as we are still happily married, I ran into the First Sergeant. This was rare for the First Sergeant to show up at this hour of the day, so I did what any good Non-Commissioned Officer would do and I showed him around the motor pool. The first thing he noticed was that there were no soldiers around. I explained that I sent them home to spend some time with their families. You could tell that he was not a fan of this idea. I still think that the reason he didn't like my idea was that his family was still in North Carolina and did not plan on moving to Kentucky until after the deployment.

The second thing he noticed was that the windows on the trucks were dusty. I remember thinking to myself that the windows were always dusty because we built a motor pool below a damn gravel pit. It turned out that the First Sergeant wouldn't be able to get any rest over the weekend if the windows were not cleaned. The First Sergeant told me to call my troops back in immediately and clean the windows. At this point my guys had already been home for over an hour. That meant half of them had already started to drink, the other half were probably out playing with their kids, and all of them would have been furious to get called back in to wash some windows. So I spent the next two hours washing each and every window on our trucks by myself.

A theme that I hope is very clear in this book is sacrifice. As a true leader you have to be selfless, or to use one of today's buzzwords, "a servant leader." (I'm not a hundred percent sure why, but I hate that phrase.) In this story, I sacrificed two hours of my time away from family before a deployment so that my guys could spend some quality time with their families. I know this is not an extraordinary sacrifice, but it was the only story that I could recall making a sacrifice for such a stupid reason.

Making sacrifices for your team usually means taking on something or shielding your people from something. This usually translates into giving up some or all your personal time for a period of time. As a leader it is important to have the right person by your side who understands the importance of making sacrifices because you are not the only one making the sacrifice. I have been lucky: the pre-deployment fling turned out to be the most supportive and understanding person in my life when it comes to making sacrifices for the team and my career. Keep in mind that not all sacrifices have to be big; sometimes the small ones mean the most to a team.

The second thing this story reminds me of is that once you hit a certain level of seniority, you seem to lose your common sense. I am still not sure why the First Sergeant even came down to the motor pool that day or why he cared so much about some dusty windows, especially because the trucks were about to sit there for a year while we were deployed. There wasn't going to be anyone left to take care of them while we were gone. Just to clarify, you would not have been able to draw any funny designs or write any obscene words on any of the windows. They were dusty but not that dusty. But for whatever reason, he was very passionate about the windows and I did what I had to do to meet his demands.

Most of the time when a senior leader makes some sort of off-the-wall request, there is usually some behind-the-scenes reason for the request that the rest of us may never know. Who knows, maybe there was a reason for this request, but I doubt I will ever figure out the value of calling in a bunch of troops prior to a deployment to wash some windows. To me, this is the worst time to bug a bunch of soldiers because they have very limited time to spend with their families before being gone for an entire year.

Chapter 17
Present Arms

"I think whether you're having setbacks or not, the role of a leader is to always display a winning attitude."

— Colin Powell

In 2008 I found myself back in Iraq with one of the best battle buddies any Sergeant could have. We were thick as thieves and rarely did anything without one another, even before this deployment. Our wives or soon-to-be wives also became close friends, and that helped out a lot as well. This deployment was not the first for either of us, so we thought we had this whole war thing figured out.

When we deployed, we had to spend about two weeks at Camp Buehring in Kuwait to get acclimated to the heat and get any new gear that we did not already have. We also had to do a three-day field exercise that was absolutely terrible. But for the most part, it was a lot of hurry up and wait with quite a bit of downtime.

One evening my battle buddy and I got a little tent crazy and decided to go for a walk to see what was going on around the base. Surprise, surprise, there was not much to do. We did, however, run into more than a few officers that night. When you encounter an officer, you have to salute their rank, and in return they salute your uniform. It is also common to sound off with the time of day followed by "Sir" or "Ma'am" or with your unit's motto.

That night we decided to sound off with either "Stay the course" or "For hearts and minds." If you recall, around this time "Stay the course" and "Winning the hearts and minds" were the major talking points that were coming out of Washington, DC. We found it to be funny and meant no disrespect to the President, the Secretary of Defense, or anyone else that was pushing the same talking points. Most of the officers we encountered that night just laughed or smiled and moved on. However, we did meet a butter bar (First Lieutenant) who did not share the same sense of humor that my battle buddy and I shared.

The Lieutenant decided that she was going to set us straight that night, and rightfully so thinking back on this story. She locked us both up at the position of attention and explained to us that as Sergeants we should know that we are doing more than winning the hearts and minds over there. Her speech was one for the record books because it went on for about five minutes without a single cuss word. (This was very unusual and uncommon for a good old-fashioned ass-chewing to not include a string of profanity.) She finally released us by saying, "Carry on," and we headed back to our tents, laughing about how the night turned out.

Later on that deployment I realized she was right to stop us and to tell us to knock it off but not for the reasons she stated. Don't get me wrong: we did do a whole hell of a lot more than win over some hearts and minds, but that isn't what she should have told us. She should have told us to knock it off because as the middle managers of the United States Army and because we had soldiers underneath us, we had to support and echo our senior leadership's vision even if we didn't agree with their vision or how they stated it.

Not every business leader is going to be the chairman of the board, or a chief executive officer who gets to create the vision for the business. Whether you are a junior supervisor or a senior vice president, we have to echo our leaders' vision to our employees in a way that makes them want to invest themselves in the project, team, department, and company. If we do not have invested employees, we will never be able to have a successful organization. As leaders, we have to build a culture of personal investment by showing our dedication in a positive way that is contagious to others.

Chapter 18
Red Man

"War is not only a matter of equipment, artillery, group troops or air force; it is largely a matter of spirit or morale."

— Chiang Kai-shek

In the fall of 2008 after a six-hour convoy, I found myself at a very small base in Iraq. It was so far out in the middle of nowhere I can't even tell you what city we were near. After the guys unloaded the cargo and got loaded back up, we were ready to head back to our home base, which was much larger and nicer.

However, the insurgents had a little different plan for us. They started to mortar the small base. Mortars were something we all were used to, and we all had the same view on them. They were not accurate at all, and if one of them got us, it was just our time to go. We really weren't too afraid of mortars, but because of how small the base was, they were hitting a little closer than normal. During this time of the war, whoever was in charge wouldn't let us leave the gate while we were taking indirect fire.

Once everything calmed down for a bit, we packed up in our trucks to head back home. At this time we were all ready to get back to Tikrit and sleep in our own beds. This time Mother Nature had other plans for us. A massive sand storm rolled in out of nowhere and kept us in place. During sand storms we were not allowed to run a convoy because the medical evacuation was grounded because helicopters cannot fly due to the sand in the air. This sand storm was a typical storm; if you held your hand out about twenty-four inches in front of you, you wouldn't be able to count your fingers. It was a good thing we were grounded because it wouldn't have been safe for us to drive in those conditions. At this time we decided to RON (rest overnight) at the base because even after the storm cleared up, our guys would have been up for over twenty-four hours, and that wasn't safe either.

None of us could go to sleep right away, and we all ended up in the MWR to get out of the sand and to hang out. The troops were very restless and started to bitch about how the night had gone. At first, I just thought it was soldiers being soldiers, but it quickly escalated out of control, and the bitching went from the events of that night to everything that was wrong with our unit and the United States Army. I knew something had to be done before this conversation got any more out of control and started to erode the high level of morale our guys usually had.

I threw in a pinch of Red Man Golden Blend (because that is all this small base had at the Post Exchange) and walked over to the table where all the troops were sitting, planning to send them all to their tents for the night. That was when one of our very good, but class-clown types said, "Hey Sergeant Ripp. I have ten dollars if you eat that whole bag of chewing tobacco." That was when the whole mood of the troops changed. Every soldier chipped in some money, and the pot got up to about eighty dollars or so.

I knew this would make me sick for a few hours, but if it would keep everyone entertained for a bit (and hopefully until they were ready to fall asleep), it would be worth it. So I said, "Bring it on." I pulled up a chair to their table and started eating. To this day, that was the worst stomachache I have ever had in my entire life! And I did not take their money. On a side note, I finished the bag, the troops went to bed laughing, and they seemed to forget about how bad the night was earlier.

I was violently sick for a few days—not just a few hours.

As leaders we are not only responsible for making decisions under pressure or making the right calls to achieve the mission or vision for the project. We are also charged with being the morale officers for our team. I have never seen an unhappy person perform at their very best. Don't get me wrong: I am not saying that we have to cater to people or that we are there for their entertainment, but if we can do something to keep our people happy and motivated, we have to do it. One thing is for sure though: I do not suggest eating a whole bag of chewing tobacco. Ever.

Chapter 19
The Shameful Mistake

*"Nobody made a greater mistake
than he who did nothing because
he could do only a little."*

— Edmund Burke

This is a story that to this day I am still ashamed to have been involved in. The nature of this story evokes some terrible feelings because roughly twenty-three of my brothers and sisters lose their battle with suicide every day. This story did not click instantly for me in some regards, but I reference and replay this story in my mind every time I have to have a tough conversation with someone.

Back in 2008 at some remote base in the middle of nowhere Iraq, one of my soldiers was struggling with some issues back home. The reason he was having issues is not important to this story, but you do need to know that the majority of the issues he was having back home were self-inflicted. My soldier came to me after the convoy and explained what was going on. He appeared very unstable, upset, and extremely irrational, so I grabbed a battle buddy and we walked my soldier to the MWR so he could call his wife back home. After about an hour-long phone call (on my calling card, I might add), my soldier walked out of the MWR in tears and only said, "I am leaving this fucking country tonight, either on an airplane on leave or in a body bag."

Emergency leave was not uncommon during this time of the war, but as you recall, I never had any luck getting it approved. You had to have your command's support for emergency leave, and that was impossible when you were a few hundred miles away from your home base and command team. I will never understand why, but at this point my battle buddy locked and loaded his rifle and handed it to my soldier. I still wish I would have reacted faster and grabbed the rifle from my battle buddy. I thank God my soldier dropped the rifle and fell to his knees. After some curse words, I pulled myself together and stripped my soldier of all weapons and ammo and immediately escorted him to the TMC (troop medical center) for mental-health treatment.

At the TMC my platoon had to pull around-the-clock suicide watch on my soldier for several days until we could get a MEDEVAC (medical evacuation) flight for him. This delayed our mission for a few days, and all my fellow NCOs took turns keeping an eye on my unstable soldier. We finally got him booked on a MEDEVAC three or four days later, and we continued on with our mission. On a side note, after my soldier got back to the States, he received additional mental-health-care treatment and was separated from the United States Army under a general discharge with Veterans Affairs benefits.

I know this is a pretty horrible story, but all of this happened very fast and I certainly did not let the lessons learned here go unnoticed. Also, if we ever worked together or if you heard me speak, you probably heard this story and my thoughts about this story because I think this is such an important, valuable lesson that everyone needs to know and understand, especially leaders.

Everyone has hard times, both professionally and personally, from time to time, and no matter how hard you try to keep things separate, they always seem to bleed into one another. With that being said, the first lesson is that you never fully know what is going on in someone else's life or how they will react to additional bad or undesirable news.

As a leader, more than likely you have people working for you, and you will also more than likely have to deliver bad news at some point during your relationship with your employees. People, especially leaders, need to be aware of the impact the news may have on the person, which is a fairly easy task to accomplish. It just takes a small investment of time and dedication to get to know your employees and what is going on in their lives, in a general sense. You can pick up on these things by reading people's body language without even saying a single word or by simply asking someone a question. To me, this is a major part of what makes the difference between a manager and a true leader.

The only thing I did correctly in this story (aside from giving my soldier my last phone card) was asking a peer and battle buddy to accompany me and my soldier to the MWR. Even though he made a very poor decision that night, a second set of eyes and ears on a situation is usually not a bad idea. Whenever I need to have a difficult conversation that I know has the potential to end poorly, I always try to have a peer or other impartial third party in the room during the conversation. This is a prime example of why as a leader you need to have a great rapport with your human resources department. They serve as a great third party for these difficult conversations. This strategy protects both the leader and the other party, and if need be, they can help defuse a volatile situation. Unfortunately, that did not happen in this story. However, with a professional human resources partner, I have never had an issue like I did in this story.

The third thing I took away from this situation is subtler and has led to a few disagreements with senior leaders, but this lesson is still true in this story and the same is true in business. If you have to take a pause to take care of your employees, the mission will still continue at some point.

In the story we were still winning the war after the surge, a few down days at a remote post did not change the outcome of the war, and it gave us some much-needed downtime off the road. In much the same way, if a leader takes a few hours to invest in an employee, it will probably not change the outcome of a project, nor will it have a negative impact on the department or the organization.

Employees are the biggest cost and resource to most organizations; therefore, they should have the most attention and resources available to help them. This only makes the department, organization, or company stronger and more competitive. Let's not forget to mention the amount of money you can save by reducing turnover by having happy employees who know their leaders are truly invested in them and their happiness in the workplace.

Chapter 20
The Helmet Throw

"Great thoughts speak only to the thoughtful mind, but great actions speak to all mankind."

— Theodore Roosevelt

Back in 2008 in Tikrit, Iraq, the entire company was called to the battalion headquarters for an awards ceremony. (Let me make a side note here. Most soldiers do not care about awards or other forms of recognition like that. Don't get me wrong: it's nice to be noticed for your hard work, but after a long night mission the last thing you want to do is get up early after a few hours—if that—of sleep to get another ribbon for a uniform that you didn't even bring to Iraq.) We were all told to load up on the five-ton truck at a set time. At that set time we had everyone except one Sergeant.

We waited a few minutes for the Sergeant to show up before his squad leader, who was a Staff Sergeant, ordered another soldier to go wake up the Sergeant. About five minutes later the Sergeant showed up half-dressed and clearly upset about the whole situation.

The Staff Sergeant said something along the lines of, "How nice of you to join us, Sergeant. Now get on the truck before we are late." The Sergeant responded with something along the lines of how he didn't care about this stupid awards ceremony. Then all hell broke loose. The Staff Sergeant who was still on the back of the five-ton and the Sergeant who was still on the ground started yelling at one another in a very unprofessional manner. Then out of nowhere the Staff Sergeant launched his ACH (army combat helmet) toward the Sergeant. This is where my battle buddy, a fellow Sergeant, and I stopped laughing, stepped in, and broke up the dispute. We put the Sergeant in the cab of the five-ton, returned the Staff Sergeant's ACH to him in the back of the five-ton, and headed off to the awards ceremony.

The awards ceremony went off without a hitch, and we all had a pretty new ribbon to hang on our dress uniforms when we returned home. When we got back to our housing area, there was a meeting with all the Sergeants and the Platoon Sergeant, a Sergeant First Class. The end result was that both the Staff Sergeant and the Sergeant who got into the screaming match were stripped of all leadership responsibilities. The Sergeant was assigned to a very undesirable paperwork position down in the motor pool, and the Staff Sergeant got moved to a totally new position in a different platoon. I fully supported all of this.

I learned a couple things from this experience. The first is that at times things are going to get a little out of hand, and the frustration is going to get to all parties. This is something we can control by our actions. The Staff Sergeant in the story didn't have to provoke the Sergeant with a smart comment. The Sergeant did not have to share his opinion about the awards ceremony in front of all the soldiers. Some of the soldiers were excited because it was their first award. Had the Sergeant just gotten on the truck and apologized for running late, I am pretty sure this story would have ended a lot differently.

The second thing I learned was that when you need to vent or blow off some steam, do it behind closed doors. Had the Sergeant waited to vent to the Staff Sergeant behind closed doors, the conversation could have gone the same way, only two people would have known how bad the conversation went, and both would have probably been able to keep their jobs. There is a time and place to vent and get your frustrations out, but in a large group with your peers and subordinates is not the best place.

The last of my takeaways from this story is that as a leader you should never send a junior person to do your job of checking on a more senior person. There were at least four Sergeants on the back of the five-ton that could have very easily gone to wake up their fellow Sergeant who was running late. Or the Staff Sergeant could have actually done his job by checking on his Sergeant. Regardless, you should never send an employee to check up on a manager. These types of situations are best handled manager to manager or senior manager to junior manager. As leaders, we have to do our job and quit being so damn lazy!

Chapter 21
Decisions

"Inability to make decisions is one of the principal reasons executives fail. Deficiency in decision-making ranks much higher than lack of specific knowledge or technical know-how as an indicator of leadership failure."

— John C. Maxwell

In 2009 I was transferred to Germany, and before I was selected to be part of the European Command Protective Services Detail, I spent a few weeks in a unit that was based out of Manheim. My wife and I were extremely excited to be stationed in Germany until we actually landed there. After our plane hit the ground, my wife and I met up with the United States Army, Germany, in-processing team who worked inside the Frankfort airport. The personnel soldier told us that our orders had changed and instead of being stationed in K-Town (Kaiserslautern), we were going to be stationed in Manheim. We then loaded up on a shuttle bus headed to Manheim. When we finally arrived, we were greeted by my new Platoon Sergeant who took us to a local hotel because the base hotel was full at the time. He did not provide a whole lot of information at this time; he did tell me though that the unit was slated for a twelve-month deployment in the coming months, but he didn't even say whether it was Iraq or Afghanistan.

I won't lie—I was burnt out on Iraq at this time. At this point I had been married for about fourteen months or so, and nine of those months I spent in Iraq, a month and a half in training, and about a month filled up with return deployment items that kept me away from my new family most nights. Needless to say, I was not looking forward to another round of deployment ramp-up training, field exercises, and being gone from my wife for yet another year. But at the end of the day, it is what it is when you volunteer to be in an army whose country is at war. You have to expect to be deployed whether you want to or not.

The next day I reported to work and had a formal meeting with the Platoon Sergeant. This is where I expected him to provide the full details of the unit, my new squad, and all the timelines for the deployment, but I was wrong. It was just a "Welcome to Germany" meeting and "Hope you like it here" type of thing. None of my questions were answered, and I was very disappointed by the lack of information that was provided. I wrote that meeting off, assuming he did not know all the details that I was seeking and that he wanted me to focus on all the in-processing to the unit, base, and country before he expected me to start working.

I spent the next two weeks drawing gear, filling out stacks of paperwork, and getting lost around my new base. I would always return to our platoon area when I was finished with my in-processing tasks, usually around 1530 (3:30 p.m.) or 1600 (4:00 p.m.), to spend some time with the troops and to get to know them better. From what I could gather, they were all great soldiers and highly motivated. The only common complaint across the junior enlisted troops was that no one could ever make a decision. I really found that odd because there were a whole lot of Sergeants that were assigned to the platoon, and most of the time Sergeants got in trouble for jumping the gun and giving orders, not sitting back and waiting on directions.

On one of the days I was in the platoon area in the afternoon, I found myself talking to a young Private and I asked him what he was doing. He told me that for the last two hours he had just been sitting around in the platoon room waiting on someone to tell him what to do. Honestly, my first thought was that he was just trying to avoid doing some work and that he was trying to hide. So I walked into the Platoon Sergeant's office to ask what was going on, trying to see what task we could assign this soldier.

The Platoon Sergeant told me that everyone was just waiting around for the workday to come to an end. So I pushed a little harder for more information to see if there was anything that needed to be done, and he told me no. I was truly baffled at the situation, and I am sure I had a dumb look on my face when I asked, "Why are we keeping the troops here if there is nothing to do?" The Platoon Sergeant explained that it was not his call to send the soldiers home, and that only the First Sergeant could release the troops. So I asked what we could have the soldiers do until they were released by the First Sergeant. He told me that he had nothing for them to do. Still baffled, I asked him what time the First Sergeant would stop by the area to release the troops. The Platoon Sergeant, who was clearly getting frustrated by all my questions, told me that the First Sergeant did not come by the platoon areas to release the soldiers. I still remember feeling like I was getting dumber by the minute as this conversation went on. After all of this, I headed home and told my wife what had happened, still in disbelief.

A few days went by, and my in-processing was winding down. I got to spend a day in the motor pool with the soldiers working on our trucks. I was still not assigned to any official position in the platoon at this time, but I couldn't sit still any longer and had to start working. While I was helping a soldier with a dead-lined truck (a truck that is not mission ready due to some mechanical defect), the Platoon Sergeant was conducting a walk-through of the motor pool. When he came over to our area, I asked him how he wanted the soldiers to proceed with the dead-lined truck. Once again, he couldn't provide me with a direct answer, and this time I refused to let myself get sucked down a rabbit hole of trying to get an answer or direction out of him. The soldier and I figured out how we could fix the truck, and with some help from a couple maintenance guys, the truck was fixed by the end of the day.

As leaders, people will always look to us for direction of some sort. If you do not get that warm feeling inside you when people seek your advice and guidance, you are in the wrong position! We should want to provide our knowledge to others, and the great leaders have a deep passion for this. Honestly, this is the major reason I get out of bed every morning and go to work. Whether it is teaching one of my sons something new or helping someone out at the office with a problem, these situations are what drive me each and every day—unlike the Platoon Sergeant in the story who was afraid or too timid to provide this type of direction.

The other takeaway from this story is that we have to be able to make a quick decision. Not making a decision is oftentimes much worse than making the wrong one. By making a decision, even a wrong decision, we have shown our team that we are not afraid to make the call to send the team down a path that made sense at the time. When we make no decision at all, we show the team that we have no faith in ourselves to make the call. If we do not have faith in ourselves, how the hell can we expect our team to have faith in us? To put this whole chapter in very simple terms, we have to step up, make decisions, and be a leader because no one will do it for us. On a side note, if you do find yourself in a position where others are making the decisions for you, I suggest that you dust off your resume and start looking for a new job because you are no longer needed in the organization.

Chapter 22
Poland

*"The truth of the matter is that you
always know the right thing to do.
The hard part is doing it."*

— Norman Schwarzkopf

As I mentioned in the introduction, as the years
went by, I achieved rank, and because of that I had
the opportunity to interview for some very specialized,
high-profile positions. The following story happened
while I was serving as the Operations NCOIC of the
European Command's Protective Service Detachment.
This was probably the best job I will ever have, or at
least the best job I have ever had up until this point in
my career.

Back in 2010 you may recall a tragic plane crash
that killed Poland's President along with several

other heads of state and other high-ranking Polish government officials. You may also remember that during this time a massive volcano was erupting in Iceland, grounding the majority of airplanes that were scheduled to cross the Atlantic Ocean. It was not melting lava that was the concern, but what the ash could do to the engine of an airplane while in flight that kept the flights grounded.

The HRP (high-risk personnel) that our team was assigned to protect were on a trip to the Pentagon along with four of our agents. They were grounded for the time being, but the HRP still had every intention of making it to Poland for the funerals. Let me give you a little background information on this: when our team was assigned a mission, we usually tried to send at least two agents to the location about a week in advance to work with the local government to identify what resources were available to us. We also liked to map out hospitals, different routes, and get a feel for the local area and culture.

My boss, the Detachment NCOIC, and I decided that we would take the mission in Poland and make the ten-hour drive to Warsaw to make all the preparations should our HRP be able to get a flight out of the States and back to Europe. Two days later, my boss and I arrived in Warsaw. I have to say, this was one of the most somber missions I have ever been on while in the military. All of Poland seemed to be grieving their loss. My boss and I checked into our hotel and blocked off a set of rooms, just in case the rest of our team, including the HRP and his entourage, were able to make the trip.

After we got everything set up at the hotel, we headed over to the United States Embassy to get briefed on the funeral plans and to meet the other teams that were on the ground from other agencies, supporting several different HRPs. The embassy suggested that we meet up with our Polish counterparts and scheduled a follow-up meeting for ten o'clock the next morning to discuss any issues or concerns we had. We were also asked to share our notes with the other teams and vice versa.

My boss and I met up with two of the most professional soldiers I have ever worked with who provided us with a map with a suggested primary route and multiple secondary routes already documented for us. We spent the next few hours running the routes and picking out our key reference points. After we felt somewhat comfortable with the routes, our counterparts took us to meet the Polish honor guard troops assigned to the funeral detail. They did a dry run of their drills that they would be doing at the funeral for us. I remember being very impressed with their skills and the discipline that it took to execute the drills flawlessly.

The next morning my boss and I discussed everything we saw from the day before and planned which items we wanted to bring up at the 1000 (10:00 a.m.) meeting at the embassy. We showed up at the embassy around 0930 (9:30 a.m.) and spent some time sipping coffee and talking to the United States Marines assigned to protect our embassy. They filled us in on the best restaurants, places we needed to see, and just the general culture of Poland. I always tried to take advantage of sightseeing and cultural experiences during a mission because I was not sure when or if I would ever make it back to Poland.

It was about ten minutes past ten o'clock when our embassy point of contact greeted us and escorted us back to his office. Our embassy point of contact told us that most of the teams were not doing anything besides drinking and having a good time because their HRPs would probably not get a flight due to the volcano. So we had our meeting, linked back up with our Polish counterparts, and continued to run mission rehearsals. We did this for the next three days, and we were the only team rehearsing.

It turned out that none of the United States HRPs were able to make the trip in time for the funerals. It was disappointing that we were not able to send a delegation to the funerals, but it was out of our control. Mother Nature always seems to win when she decides to put up a fight.

The first lesson is something that I have to work on every day—much like most leaders—and it is not an easy task for me. The lesson is simply letting things go that are out of your control. As a leader, you probably want everything to go smoothly for your effort and your team. However, at times things will not go as planned, and during some of these times—a loss of data, a loss of a key teammate, an illness that someone catches, or just about any natural disaster—there is nothing you can do about it. I am sure the local leaders in Joplin, Missouri, or the areas affected by Hurricane Katrina have a lot more heroic stories about when things do not go as planned, but as a leader you have to shake it off and move forward to recover the current task or to make sure you don't have the same issues for the next mission.

The second lesson was the most powerful one from this story in my opinion: individual actions can change how another person or organization views your organization as a whole. We all knew that there was a slim-to-no chance that our HRPs would be able to make the trip to Poland. However, there was still a small chance, and my boss and I were not going to embarrass ourselves or our HRP if that chance became a reality. We ran the mission the same way we would have run the mission if there was a hundred percent chance of arrival. I wish I could have said the same for the other agencies that had agents on the ground. By blowing off the meeting and not running rehearsals, they not only embarrassed themselves, their agencies, and their HRPs, they embarrassed all of us as a nation by not showing respect to an ally nation during their time of mourning. I am sure most Polish citizens understood that our leaders could not make the trip for reasons that were out of their control. But I know for a fact that the Polish soldiers I worked with could not understand why the other agencies were not taking the mission seriously.

This is why, while on business or personal travel, I always do my best to maintain a professional posture. You never know who may see you at an airport or hotel bar. Like it or not, you are always representing something bigger than yourself. Sometimes you are just a representative of your department, such as at a company function. Other times you will find yourself representing the company as a whole at an industry conference or similar event. Sometimes you may even find yourself representing your country. This is something you cannot afford to screw up or take lightly. It is nearly impossible to recover from bad impressions.

Chapter 23
The Mentor

"Tell me and I forget, teach me and I may remember, involve me and I learn."

— Benjamin Franklin

This story is pulled from several other chapters including "Poland" and "New Job," and the person in the story was referenced in "The General." This is about one of the best leaders I have ever had the opportunity to serve under, just like the General later on in this book.

Back in 2010 I created my own position as the Operation NCOIC of the European Command Protective Services Detachment. The Detachment NCOIC was a Sergeant First Class. At first, I did not think much of him because he had served eighteen years and never deployed. This was very rare—to have served during such a long war and never deployed. At this time I had been in for only about six years and already spent more time than I care to mention deployed. Right or wrong, that was my first opinion of this specific Sergeant First Class.

It did not take long for my opinions to change about the Sergeant First Class. We had a shared office, and our desks were about ten feet away from each other at a maximum. We ate lunch together every day, and we almost always talked shop. We would discuss which agents we were sending on which missions and why we selected certain agents for specific protection missions. We would also swap stories about what we had done on past assignments. My stories were usually about being deployed because I knew he knew nothing about that. His stories were things that he did that he thought got him to the rank of Sergeant First Class. He truly wanted to see all of us have a better career than he had and was always looking for a way to share his knowledge.

The biggest thing I learned from this Sergeant First Class was professionalism. I was doing alright on my own to get a position in such a highly visible unit, but he took me to a whole new level. In my other assignments I had to interact with a lot of people but never with anyone who held an office of high power or status until this position. (Keep in mind we were charged with protecting the Supreme Allied Commander of European Forces—NATO, and any high-level visitors they had. Not to name-drop but to show the level of leaders we worked with, we protected the Secretary of Defense, State Department officials, the Joint Chiefs of

Staff, and the Chief of Staff for all service components when they visited us in Stuttgart, Germany.) It takes a special kind of finesse to successfully interact with leaders of such high status, and the Sergeant First Class taught me not only how to interact with them but how to leave a positive impression on them. This led to several of our frequent visitors specifically asking for certain agents to be assigned to them when they returned.

I could go on and on about how he turned me from a professional soldier who craved being deployed with his troops to a professional who could interact with some of the highest-ranking officials our country has. I could never repay him for all the things he taught me.

I think the title of this chapter gives away what I am about to talk about in the next few paragraphs, but it is such an important message. As the Detachment NCOIC, the only responsibility the Sergeant First Class really had was to make sure that I had the resources to assign and execute missions and that all the soldiers were doing what they should be doing. However, his required tasks were only a small portion of what he actually did. They become kind of a secondary task for him. He saw his value to the detachment as a true leader and to pass on his knowledge.

For any leader—whether a business leader, coach, politician, military officer, or NCO—this is a skill and an investment we have to make in our people. Is it really all that hard to put in a little extra effort to develop our people? The value that a well-developed employee can provide is exponentially more than an average employee who has not been mentored. It is easy to do the bare minimum required by our position, but if that is all we do, we will get only bare minimum results.

The reason I believe this relationship was so successful is that there was a level of trust that was built during our time together. Remember, I was not impressed with him when we first met because he had not deployed. I could have let that initial feeling stick with me, but I went into the relationship with an open mind. Who knows what his first impression was of me, but he also had to have an open mind or I would have never ended up in the position that I held. Relationships are invaluable in all aspects of life, but the relationships that are built on mutual respect, trust, faith, and confidence can change your life.

The last lesson that I learned from this story is one that we all need to know if we want to reach our full potential: we have to seek knowledge. The Sergeant First Class was always seeking to pass on his knowledge, but the majority of the time I came to him with questions when I needed a little guidance. In the cut-throat culture of corporate America, we are not always going to have someone go out of their way to share and pass on their experiences to us. We have to seek the information that we need. We have to take control and seek to build these relationships with the people we work with.

It is also valuable to have outside mentors as well. The outside mentor brings a unique perspective to the situation because they are not emotionally attached to anything that is going on inside your organization. They can provide advice solely on the facts. I firmly believe that as leaders we need both internal and external mentors to bring out our full potential.

Chapter 24
Small World

"A small world where people know each other, and still so deep, able to get lost."

— Anthony Liccione

Most people know that the United States military is a fairly small community, and it is not uncommon to run into others that you have served with from time to time. Whether it was a school you attended or a unit that you were assigned to, you will more than likely run into that person again in your career. This story is similar but not exactly the same.

In 2010 I was assigned to a very nice three-week protective service mission in Naples, Italy. It was actually two missions with just three days in between the two, so it was cheaper to leave me in Naples than it was to fly me back and forth twice. I didn't mind spending a couple extra days eating pizza and gelato on the Italian coast. The wine didn't suck either. I was also able to fly my wife down for the three-day break. Overall, it was just a fun, enjoyable trip.

It was a typical mission where the advance team showed up and ran routes with the Carabinieri (the National Military Police of Italy). We walked the facilities that we knew our HRP was going to visit, as well as the surrounding areas where he might want to stop. The HRP showed up on time, and every aspect of the mission went smoothly for the first leg.

After the first mission, my wife flew down, and we spent the next few days bumming around Naples and Pompeii. We also ate like it was our last day on Earth. We did all the typical touristy things, and we got some of the best pictures taken of us. It was another smooth few days and a total blast to share the experience of the area with her.

You are probably thinking that something crazy happened on the third leg of this mission. Well, you would be wrong. Everything went smoothly for us, and we even got to see the Carabinieri beat the hell out of the hood of a Ferrari with a stop stick because the driver did not stop quickly enough for their liking. (Just a general life lesson learned here ... if you ever find yourself in Italy, do not mess with the Carabinieri! I cannot stress that enough.)

On the final night of the mission, our HRP flew out, and we stayed at the airport the required time in case his flight was turned around. After we were cleared to leave the airport, we headed out for our wheels-up dinner. (Wheels-up parties became famous after some protection agencies took things a little too far, like in Colombia, for example. Ours were a lot less extravagant and borderline boring compared to other agencies.) We headed to a restaurant on the Amalfi Coast where our HRP ate and one that he highly recommended. This just happened to be one of the best restaurants that I have ever had the opportunity in which to dine. It had the most breathtaking view, and it was located right on the banks of the coast. If you are ever bored, Google the Amalfi Coast. The pictures are absolutely beautiful.

We had two teams; one was based in Shape, Belgium, and my team was based out of Stuttgart, Germany. During this dinner I was talking to an agent who was new to the Shape team. (We were more creative with our team name; we were known as the Stuttgart team.) During my chat with the newly assigned agent, we discovered that we were both from southwest Ohio. As we dug down deeper, it turned out we both went to the same little Catholic high school, just a few years apart from one another. We joked about how many water-main breaks we had that led to a day off school. (Our school had some serious water-main issues, but they seemed to flare up only on the day after a major sporting event, like the time our hockey team made it to the national tournament, or when our girls' basketball team made it to the state finals.) It was a great night going down memory lane, and the great food and gorgeous view were icing on the cake.

This mission was just a fun three weeks for me. However, after that wheels-up dinner, I started to think back to the time I spent at the small Catholic high school. I had a blast back in high school. Because of that and several other reasons, I chose to enlist in the United States Army rather than immediately going off to college. While I was out having too much fun and not spending enough time with my head in the books, I created a reputation for myself—a reputation that was less than desirable and one that I am not proud of to this day. Luckily for me, there were a few years difference between me and the other agent in this story, so we knew a lot of the same people but didn't really know each other. That night all I could think about was how different that conversation would have been had he known me back in high school. I am proud to say that by the time we officially met, I had already pulled my head out of the place it was back in high school.

To this day I always try to conduct myself in a manner that will lead to a reputation that I can be proud of, not only as a leader but as a person. I cannot think of one leader I have ever worked with or served under that I respected as a leader but not as a person. Like it or not, you create your reputation with your own actions. Your leadership skills are judged on your actions and your reputation. As a leader you must think about your decisions, focus on how you want to be perceived, and execute through your actions. You never know when you will have a blast from the past with someone halfway around the world.

Chapter 25
The General

"If your actions inspire others to
dream more, learn more, do more
and become more, you are a leader."

— John Quincy Adams

We all have leaders in our past that we enjoyed working for, and they will always hold a special place in our hearts for what they taught us, sometimes without even realizing that they were teaching us. I am lucky enough to have served with two of these leaders in my military career. One was the Sergeant First Class that you read about a little earlier in the "The Mentor," but this story covers one small mission with a Three Star Lieutenant General who taught me a great lesson.

Due to his position, this General was authorized a full protection detail that included an armed PSO

(Protective Services Operator), a driver, and a chase car with at least two additional armed agents. However, all the General ever took with him was an unarmed driver. I was not permanently assigned to this General, but I was his backup driver. He also happened to be from Ohio, and most Buckeye fans hit it off right away. With that connection, it made for some fun football conversations in the car.

I remember this mission like it was yesterday because I had just gotten home from an assignment outside Germany, and my wife and I had plans. When this mission came down and the General's primary driver was on a different mission, I got assigned to it. It was a Saturday, and the only details I had about the mission were that I was going to pick up the General and his aide at his residence and we were going to Heidelberg, which is about a two-hour drive. This was not uncommon for the General to operate like this; his aide was very good about giving directions, so it was not a huge deal.

When I picked up the General, he and his aide were in civilian clothes. This, however, was uncommon for the two. I should mention that during this time of my career, it was very uncommon for me to don my military uniform. I was usually in a suit and tie, but the dress code for this mission was khakis and a polo shirt. This did not bother me one bit, mostly because I am not a fan of wearing ties. On the way up to Heidelberg, the General was working and his aide filled me in that we were going to give a tour of the Schloss Castle. I enjoyed visiting castles, and I was excited about the tour—so excited that I never once thought to ask to whom we were giving the tour.

We arrived early, as usual, and walked around the square at the base of the castle while we waited for our guest. I was more than a little shocked when a white Greyhound-style bus showed up full of patients along with some medical staff. I finally got around to asking the General's aide who we were giving the tour to. He informed me that about every month or so the General cleared his calendar and personally paid for a bus full of patients and medical staff from Landstuhl Medical Center to make the trip to Heidelberg, and he gave them a personal tour of the castle. He also told me that I better not let any of the patients find out he was a General or that he personally paid for everything, or he would have to kill me. The aide was Special Forces qualified, so I just assumed he was serious and kept my mouth shut.

The tour was amazing, and I was very impressed by how much the General knew about the Schloss Castle. After the tour, we spent a couple hours walking around the square, visiting shops, and listening to the wounded soldiers, the majority of whom were injured in combat, tell their stories. It was one of the most rewarding days I had while serving in the United States Army.

As a leader you have probably had a very successful career with great opportunities in front of you, and you will more than likely progress even further as the years go by. At a certain point we have to give back. Giving back doesn't have to be as big as bussing thirty-plus people to a beautiful castle a few hours away. It can be as simple as taking your team out to lunch, or holding a town-hall-style meeting to answer any questions your employees may have. There are so many ways to give back that I simply cannot list them all here. Find what works for you and what you are comfortable doing and execute as often as possible.

Giving back is multifaceted. First and foremost you are doing something good for someone else or another organization. Second, it feels damn good to use your knowledge, power, position, influence, or whatever the case may be to help others. The last subject I am going to touch on is reputation. Good deeds do not go unnoticed. For proof of this, just check out glassdoor. com or any other website where people can provide reviews on a company. You can read hundreds of thousands of reviews, both positive and negative, about an organization. I have not done a 100 percent analysis of the reviews, but the best reviews I have read mention something about how the company took care of their employees. This is a great example of companies giving back to their employees, and that translates to a better reputation.

Giving back to your local community is also another important way to give back. If you can afford to sponsor a sports team, go for it! It shows that you, as a company, are committed to the community, plus you can also get some very cheap repetitive advertising. If you cannot afford something along those lines, you can do something as simple as picking up trash around your building or the road where you are located a few times a year. Commitment to employees and the local community is what separates the great companies from the average or good companies—along with strong leadership, of course.

Chapter 26
The IG Investigation

"Promise yourself to be just as enthusiastic about the success of others as you are about your own."

— Christian D. Larson

In the winter of 2010, I was still the Operation NCOIC of the European Command Protective Services Detachment. We had one of the best soldiers I have ever served with assigned to our detachment as a headquarters building guard. He was a Specialist at this time, and all our agents who traveled with the high-ranking officials had to be a Sergeant or higher. So he was not able to be an agent, but we were still able to send him to the Protective Agent Academy at Fort Leonard Wood, Missouri, to get him certified as an agent. There is a very easy explanation for this: the majority of positions in the military are based on rank and not ability. However, most of the time (but not every time) rank is equivalent to ability.

The holiday season was always the busiest time for our team because our boss wasn't allowed to leave his house without a team of agents, based on his position. In 2010 we had so many missions that I simply ran out of agents to send on all of those assignments. We did have a couple agents who were going to be transferred to us during the holiday rush, but the Detachment NCOIC and I wanted to vet and assess the new agents' capabilities and professionalism before sending them out on a mission with our HRP. They also needed time to get settled into a new location and country. We were left with no other options besides pulling up the junior soldier who had already proved his professionalism and ability during his time protecting the headquarters. The Detachment NCOIC took the soldier over to the base tailor to get a couple suits while I booked his travel and hotel in the States for the mission.

Our decision to pull the soldier up sent some waves throughout our team. Some of the senior agents did not think that the young soldier had enough experience. They thought they could do a leap-frog approach to support the follow-on mission that was assigned to the soldier. However, one flight delay or cancellation and we wouldn't have an agent on the ground to support the mission, and we would have failed with that approach. Because our team and mission were so visible to the command, failure was never an option for the Detachment NCOIC or myself. Our pride also played a role as to why we refused to fail.

Despite all the internal flak that we took, we still sent the soldier on the mission as an agent. About halfway through the mission, I got a call from the young soldier who informed me that everything was going great and that the other agents seemed to be impressed with him and his ability to protect the boss. He also told me that he found a very cheap flight from his location in Florida to his home state of New York and asked if he could take some leave back home because he was already in the States. I discussed this with the Detachment NCOIC because, at the end of the day, it was his call on whether or not to approve the soldier's leave. After a short discussion, neither one of us saw an issue with his request. We were also able to save the government $300 by flying him back to Germany from New York rather than Florida.

In my opinion this was a win-win-win. The first win was that this young soldier stepped up and proved that he was more than capable to serve as an agent, and he proved that our assessment of him was correct. The second win was that a soldier who hadn't been home in almost three years was able to spend part of the holidays back home with his family. The third win was that we were able to save $300 in our travel budget that was always tight. All in all, I thought it was one of the best decisions I was part of at the time.

This is where the story should end and where I should tell you how important it is to take care of your people, but that is simply not the case. One of the senior agents was still not happy that we sent this soldier on the mission, and this agent was definitely not happy that we let him take leave after the mission. I should add that due to the high volume of travel, the Detachment NCOIC and I usually gave every agent several days off after every mission to decompress and to take care of anything that might have popped up in their personal life. Approving this soldier's leave was not uncommon or out of the norm at all. However, the senior agent did not care about the norms or how many times we took care of him after a mission. He felt that he had to report the Detachment NCOIC, our civilian advisor, and me to the Inspector General (IG) to see if we broke any laws or military regulations.

The IG opened an investigation on all three of us. The IG interviewed all the soldiers and agents that were assigned to the detachment, but never got around to asking us why we did what we did—or any other questions for that matter. After about three weeks into the investigation, the IG closed their investigation, and the only thing they found was that we did not follow the proper procedures for signatures on the soldier's leave form. Not a huge deal at all, but it still ended with a couple letters of reprimands for the detachment leadership team.

The main lesson I learned here comes from the very catty senior agent. As a professional and, quite frankly, as a person in general, we cannot be upset by others' success. In fact, we should celebrate others' successes and learn from them. I have never met a successful person who attributes their success to studying people who only failed or who claimed they did it all on their own without any help from others. There is absolutely no reason to try to go after or complain about someone who has achieved something earlier in life than you did.

The most frustrating thing to me in this story is that we were all on the same team, charged with the same mission, so the whole team was responsible for the success of the young soldier. We all trained him in our areas of focus, and he was very successful because of the training he was provided and his personal ability to absorb and retain what he was taught. This should have been a major win for the team and inspirational to the other junior enlisted soldiers we had in the detachment. Instead, it ended with an IG investigation. This had the soldiers and agents picking sides and was killing the upbeat morale of the detachment.

I also learned that if you have a question about what your leadership is doing, be an adult and ask them their reasoning when the time and place are appropriate instead of running to a third-party investigative unit. Don't get me wrong: if you suspect criminal or ethical wrongdoing, please report the incident to the proper authorities. However, do not waste their limited resources because you are bitter that some younger person stepped up, was successful, and received the same treatment as all the other agents. There is no place for this kind of jealousy in a professional environment.

The last thing that stuck with me from this experience was that no matter what is going on or how busy we get, we have to follow policies and procedures. They are there for a reason, even if we do not understand why. I still feel that a letter of reprimand was overkill for approving a soldier's leave then catching the paperwork up after the fact, but it did violate policy. There is a fine line between getting things done and making sure that all the I's are dotted and the T's are crossed and in line with the policies. At the end of the day, both are very crucial to running a successful organization.

Chapter 27
Career Ending

"If you don't know where you are going, you'll end up someplace else."

— Yogi Berra

We all encounter situations that are just out of our control. The following story is about when my military career came to grinding halt.

It was a very rainy late fall day in Germany when my wife and I made the two-hour drive to Laundstuhl Medical Center to get my leg looked at again. (I tore it up pretty good back in 2009 in Iraq.) I remember the drive very clearly. We laughed and joked the whole way up, just like young couples do. We arrived at the hospital and got lost on the base, something that happens to us both more than we care to admit. Not much changed when we entered the hospital. Once again, we found ourselves laughing about how silly it was that we always got lost. Thankfully though, we were extremely early and weren't too worried about it. We finally found our way to the correct area and signed in.

I know a lot of people think the military has great health care, but all hospitals are run the same. We had to wait in a lobby just like everyone else, and that day was no exception—it was about an hour past our appointment time before we saw the doctor. Things went well during the exam and X-ray process. I was guessing we just made a very long drive for the United States Army cure-all prescription of 800 milligrams of Ibuprofen. Unfortunately, that was not the case.

After the X-rays, the doctor came back into the exam room with a very different demeanor. He explained that more damage was done to my leg than the doctor who treated me in Iraq thought, and that my leg did not heal properly. I remember thinking, "Easy fix, right? Do your doctor thing and I will be fine." Once again, I was wrong. The doctor explained that there was nothing he could do but inject my ankle with some drugs for the pain. He also said we could try an experimental treatment where they basically inject a rubber compound into the joint. Inserting anything experimental and rubber into my body did not sit too well with me, so we opted for the drugs to see how that would go. At this point it started to sink in that I might not serve the thirty-plus years that I once dreamt I would.

Two weeks later, I was back in the same level of pain as I had been prior to that trip, so we went back for another round of shots. However, they can give this type of treatment only so many times a year, and unlucky for me, it was not twenty-six. At this time the doctor referred me to what is known as a Medical Review Board (MRB)—not a place for a highly motivated soldier.

I spent two days at a different hospital getting everything from my hair to my toes checked out. After all the exams, a report was compiled and submitted to some sort of team in Washington, DC, for a determination. A few weeks later, it was determined that I was no longer physically able to continue serving our great nation. To this day, it still stands as one of the worst moments in my professional career.

The next few months I spent turning in my gear, gathering records, and out-processing my unit and the base. We also shipped our car and damn near everything else we owned back to the States. We had to use my dad's address for everything because we did not have a house, job, or anything else back home at this time. Needless to say, it was an extremely stressful time for my wife and me.

From the day I got notified that I was no longer able to serve, I made a personal vow to myself to always have a backup plan. I did not have a plan, and if it wasn't for my family, who knows what would have happened to my wife and me. Because of my family, I can say we did not hit rock bottom, but my wife and I damn near did. A simple plan could have helped us avoid this problem that we were facing.

During this time of transition, my wife and I also found out that we were expecting our first son. Based on his due date, we realized very fast that our military insurance was going to expire about two months before he was due to be born. I couldn't find a good job with medical benefits at this time either and ended up working several odd jobs that really had no future. My wife also took a job at a restaurant to help us make ends meet. Between working multiple jobs, I was also going back to school at night because the feedback I got from the couple real interviews I had was that my lack of formal education was the sole reason I was not selected for the position. I cannot even put into words the level of stress I felt at this time. Not being able to give your spouse and children the life you want them to have is the worst feeling I have ever felt in my entire life.

Like I said in the introduction, I was not (and am still not, to be totally honest) a huge fan of formal education. I did not have a degree when I got out of the Army, and that was a major roadblock to finding employment. If I had a backup plan when I entered the United States Army, I would have taken advantage of the tuition reimbursement because a degree would have definitely been part of the plan.

We all know things do not always go the way we envision them going. We have to give it our all to make things go the way we want, but we also need a plan B and sometimes even a plan C. Can you think of one thing that went exactly the way you planned? Somewhere between the start and the finish line at some point in the process things will change. With a solid backup plan you can be as prepared as possible when you need fall back a bit and take another look.

The thing about backup plans for our lives is that we have to ensure that the backup plan keeps us on the path to reach our vision for what we want in life. I could have very easily continued to work the low-level odd jobs I was doing just to make enough to survive. Or I could have worked those jobs as a means to an end while I continued down my personal path to a successful, more meaningful mission in life. As I stated in the chapter on goals, we must always stay focused on the end goal, and we must also have multiple paths to achieve everything that we want in life. One path is just not going to cut it.

Open Letter to Hiring Managers and Employers

To whom it may concern:

I hope my book has illustrated the journey that all veterans have gone on during their time in the service. We are all exposed to great and poor leadership that has helped shape us into the leaders we are today. We learned these lessons under the pressure of life-and-death situations and not in the safety of a classroom or in a place of business.

I realize that a veteran will not always suit your hiring needs, and I am fully understanding of this. I just hope that you do not overlook a qualified veteran for employment at your place of business due to a lack of formal education. I assure you that most veterans have learned far more during their time of service than most who have a fancy piece of paper with the president of the university's signature in the bottom right hand corner. They have earned an education second to none in the real world with real bullets flying over their heads.

I hope this book was an eye-opener, that it brought to light the things veterans learn on a daily basis that do not always come out in an interview. This knowledge is invaluable to most organizations, and I hope that you as a hiring manager will take the time to consider the value in a veteran that is not always documented.

Thank you again for reading my book. I truly hope this helps you on your next hire.

Nicholas R. Ripplinger

References

Basic Training
http://thinkexist.com/quotes/tiorio/

The Board
http://www.brainyquote.com/search_results.html?q=preperation

Burnt Out
http://leadership.uoregon.edu/resources/quotes

Career Ending
http://www.goodreads.com/quotes/tag/planning

Decision
http://www.brainyquote.com/search_results.html?q=maxwell+inability+to+make

DUI Night
http://www.brainyquote.com/quotes/authors/s/sydney_j_harris.html

The Essay
http://www.positivelypositive.com/quotes/setting-goals-is-the-first-step-in-turning-the-invisible-into-the-visible/

Formation
http://www.brainyquote.com/quotes/quotes/p/peterguber503219.html?src=t_face-to-face

FTX
http://thinkexist.com/quotation/the_people_when_rightly_and_fully_trusted_will/180749.html

The General
http://www.themilitaryleader.com/resource-recommendations/quotes/

Grid Squares
http://www.leadershipnow.com/relationshipsquotes.html

The Helmet Throw
http://www.brainyquote.com/quotes/keywords/actions_speak.html

The IG
http://www.goodreads.com/quotes/189796-promise-yourself-to-be-so-strong-that-nothing-can-disturb

Introduction
http://www.motivational-inspirational-corner.com/getquote.html?categoryid=16

Mentor
http://www.goodreads.com/quotes/tag/mentoring

The Move
http://www.brainyquote.com/quotes/quotes/g/georgespa138200.html

New Job
http://www.brainyquote.com/search_results.html?q=peter+McWilliams+

Ottie
http://startupquotes.startupvitamins.com/post/117531572992/i-truly-believe-that-if-you-take-care-of-your

Perception
http://www.brainyquote.com/quotes/quotes/r/
robertfrip320743.html

Poland
http://www.motivational-inspirationalcorner.com/
getquote.html?startrow=1&categoryid=16

Present Arms
http://www.brainyquote.com/quotes/authors/c/colin_
powell.html

Red Man
http://www.azquotes.com/author/8355-Chiang_Kai_
shek

The Shameful Mistake
http://www.brainyquote.com/search_results.
html?q=burke+nobody+made

Sleeping Pills
https://www.pinterest.com/pin/100486635408277254/

Small World
http://www.goodreads.com/quotes/tag/small-world

Waiver to Deploy
http://www.goodreads.com/quotes/175910-ten-
soldiers-wisely-led-will-beat-a-hundred-with-out

Wash Rack in Iraq
http://www.themilitaryleader.com/resource-
recommendations/quotes/

Washing Windows
http://www.brainyquote.com/quotes/quotes/m/
maxdepree100557.html

Connect with Nick:

Website: www.NickRipplinger.com

Email: Nick@NickRipplinger.com

LinkedIn: https://www.linkedin.com/in/nicholas-ripplinger-14160823

Facebook: www.facebook.com/nick.ripplinger.39

Twitter: @NickRipplinger

In Gratitude

I am truly thankful that you took the time to pick up and read my book. I hope you enjoyed the time you spent with it and that you found something that will mold you into a better leader. I hope that reading this helps keep you on your personal path to a successful, meaningful mission in life.

I would be very grateful if you could take a moment out of your day to provide honest feedback on what you loved about this book on our Amazon sales page.

Again, thank you!

Nicholas R. Ripplinger

Acknowledgements

This book wouldn't have been possible without the help and support of so many people. I could probably write a whole book on just the people who have helped me to get to this point in my life.

First, I want to thank my beautiful, talented, loving, supportive wife. There were several nights where she took care of our two boys by herself so that I could focus on writing (or rewriting) portions of this book. I would not have been able to finish without her!

Second, I would like to thank my parents, Paul Ripplinger and Betsy Westhafer, and my grandparents, Silas and Juanita, and James and Dorothy, for raising me and providing me with the foundation to be a leader. I am sure they all have some gray hairs because of me, but they stood by me and all my shenanigans and taught me to learn from my mistakes. I cannot thank them enough for the way they raised me.

This book idea wouldn't have been possible if it wasn't for the opportunity I had to server under and beside some of the best soldiers and leaders in the United States Army. It was truly a pleasure to have served with you all. A few of the stories wouldn't have been possible without some of the not-so-great leaders I served with. Thank you for teaching me how a lack of leadership has a negative impact on people. This has shown me the value that good leaders can have on people's lives.

There were several others who kept me motivated on the end goal of finishing this book. There were others who helped turn my ideas into something publishable. I would like to recognize Dan and Paula Wathen and Rachel Kennedy for being champions to me on both of these fronts. Thank you both very much!

Finally, I want to thank Berny and September Dohrmann for allowing me to attend a CEO Space Forum on a weekend VIP pass. This is where I was connected to so many great thought leaders. This is also where I was introduced to my publisher, Robbin Simons, who brought this book to life. Without these three people and the magic that happens at CEO Space, this book would be just a bunch of handwritten words in my notebook.

About Nick Ripplinger

Nicholas Ripplinger enlisted in the United States Army Reserves as a Military Police Officer at the age of seventeen. Due to his young age when he chose to serve our country, a waiver signed by both of his parents was required before he could proudly take his oath. He attended basic training at Fort Leonard Wood, Missouri, between his junior and senior years of high school. After graduating high school, he enlisted in the Active Duty US Army. Nick was stationed at Fort Lee, Virginia, and Fort Knox, Kentucky; he deployed to Iraq from both of these duty stations. He also served from a base in Stuttgart, Germany.

Nick advanced through the enlisted ranks faster than most of his peers and was hand selected for several high-profile positions, such as the Division Commander's After Action Briefer for the Multi-National Forces Iraq-North. He was selected over fifty other Non-Commissioned Officers for this position. Nick was also selected as the European Command Protective Services Operations Non-Commissioned Officer in Charge where he was awarded the Defense Meritorious Service Medal, the third-highest peacetime award. He was also awarded several other medals, ribbons, awards, coins, and certificates.

Nick suffered a combat-related injury in Iraq in 2009 and fought through his injury for two more years before being medically retired from the US Army in 2011.

Since his transition to civilian life, Nick has continued to work within the Department of Defense industry supporting the war fighter back home in Ohio. Nick is passionate about helping veterans in transition, particularly as it relates to leveraging the skills gained in the business world. He is committed to changing and saving lives through his personal experiences from his military and private-sector careers.

Nick is currently raising his two beautiful sons with his lovely wife, Leah, at their small family farm in Germantown, Ohio.

Made in the USA
Middletown, DE
08 September 2017